respect-me
R·U·L·E·S

respect-me
R·U·L·E·S

Michael J. Marshall, PhD &
Shelly Marshall, BS, CSAC

Bonneville Books
Springville, Utah

ISBN 13: 978-1-59955-440-2

Published by Bonneville Books, an imprint of Cedar Fort, Inc., 2373 W. 700 S., Springville, UT 84663
Distributed by Cedar Fort, Inc. www.cedarfort.com

LIBRARY OF CONGRESS CATALOGING-IN-PUBLICATION DATA

Marshall, Michael J., 1949-
  Respect me rules : a guide to stopping verbal and emotional abuse /
Michael J Marshall and Shelly Marshall.
    p. cm.
  ISBN 978-1-59955-440-2
  1. Psychological abuse. I. Marshall, Shelly. II. Title.

  RC569.5.P75M36 2010
  616.85'82--dc22

  2010019411

Cover design by Angela D. Olsen
Cover design © 2010 by Lyle Mortimer
Edited and typeset by Kimiko Christensen Hammari and Kelley Konzak

Printed in the United States of America

10 9 8 7 6 5 4 3 2 1

Printed on acid-free paper

CONTENTS

A NOTE TO THE READER

DEALING WITH DOMESTIC VIOLENCE is beyond the scope of this book. We only address domestic abuse that does not include physical violence. If your relationship has progressed to domestic violence, then you should seek professional help. Once the abuse has turned physical, it is too late—even unsafe—to use these methods to stop the abuse. However, this book can and will help you in the event that your next partner shows signs of being an abuser—stopping abuse at the outset, when it is still in either the verbal or the emotional stage and has not yet progressed to physical violence.

Also keep in mind that we use gender neutral terms where we can because abuse is not limited to men abusing women. However, as explained in Chapter 4, "for simplicity's sake, we generally use the traditional scenario of the male abusing the female. This in no way minimizes or fails to recognize any other gender combination of abuse. This book is simply about stopping abuse in its tracks and enforcing the Respect-Me Rules, which applies to any type of couple."

INTRODUCTION

THE PERSON WHO FIGURES OUT HOW abusers can so precisely hone in on their targets should win a Nobel Prize. It's as if a large, red bull's-eye is painted on a vulnerable person's back and an abuser can zero in on the target. Nobody knows exactly what the signals are, but abusers can sense them as a lion senses prey. There undoubtedly are signals on many different levels, such as body language, tone of voice, type of response, and use of words. We've all seen the difference between a chronic victim and someone who may look small and weak but is a real dynamo. People quickly learn not to tread on the dynamo. What makes these two potential victims so different?

A basic principle of the abuse dynamic is that we teach other people how to treat us. For instance, one of the authors of this book, Shelly, was involved in a verbally abusive relationship. Following years of suffering and drama, she finally had an epiphany. After intense self-examination, she realized that she had laid herself on a silver platter for her ex-husband to abuse her. During courtship, Shelly displayed her willingness to sacrifice everything for him and took care of him and every detail of their lives, leaving him free to do as he pleased. She even went as far as to allow his guitar-playing hobby and anything else he wanted to take priority over her own career. She taught him that his needs predominated and that he came first. If he was displeased, she scrambled to fix it. Shelly explains her moment of clarity:

> Realizing I not only married a self-centered rageaholic but also that I trained him to think that it was okay to mistreat me wasn't my finest moment. However, one positive thing that came out of it was the motivation to write this book. My epiphany day in April 2003 was the beginning and the end of many things. It was the beginning of understanding why my husband felt entitled to be mean and hostile to his wife. It was the beginning of understanding why I stayed and put up with his self-absorbed lifestyle. And just as that discovery marked the beginning of understanding the

part I played in allowing abuse to continue, it also marked the end of my marriage. It didn't end because I stopped trying. I was either too stubborn or too stupid to throw in the towel. When I started using the Respect-Me Rules, my husband realized I wouldn't accept any blame, anger, or abuse one second longer. His desires no longer trumped mine. He couldn't cope with a fair partnership and demanded a divorce.

This book is different from other abuse books because we don't see the abused person as a victim, survivor, or powerless partner in the relationship. We think of the abused person as more of a target than a victim. Other books often encourage the victim to leave the relationship and get away from the abuser. We think a superior choice is to try to stop the abuse within the relationship. Only if this fails is it time to consider ending the relationship. Surprisingly, if the target uses the abuse-stopping methods we offer but the relationship is not salvageable, the abuser will often decide to leave first and save the target the trouble!

> "I eventually attended an abuse class and learned about 'my contribution' to all of it. At first it was hard to listen to. But, unlike any therapist I had in the past, the lady who taught the class got through to me. I had some changing to do!"
>
> **—DEBBIE M.**

In this book we will present a number of strategies to stop verbal and emotional abuse. If your efforts thus far have been unsuccessful, then taking a new approach makes sense. However, it will not be easy. No change is, yet your effort should pay off with big dividends. In order to grow, mature, and recover, you will need to go through developmental stages. The stages of working through abuse include denial, anger, blame, depression, and the choice of acquiescence or action. The last stage is the essence of our work. Targets can *choose* to make effective changes, such as using and enforcing the Respect-Me Rules, which should result in visible progress.

We encourage you to stop using the terms *victim* and *survivor*. They are not solution-oriented words, and the language of victimology can contribute to the problem. When you call yourself a victim, you give all the power to the perpetrator. Children are the true victims. They really *are* powerless. You're not. You're an adult. That's why we don't use the word *victim*. Once you move away from the victim mentality, we can show you that it is not necessary to adapt to an unhappy relationship. With the courage to change and the resources to light the way, a return to a happy, satisfying relationship is possible!

CHAPTER 1

You're a Target, Not a Victim

Never be bullied into silence.
Never allow yourself to be made a victim.
—HARVEY FIERSTEIN

CHANCES ARE, IF YOU ARE READING this book, you feel your partner is abusing you. There is more public awareness now about abuse in all types of relationships, especially physical abuse. However, both verbal and emotional abuse still too often lurk in the shadows because they are easier to hide. There are no visible bruises, broken arms, black eyes, or hospital reports to evidence your pain. And professionals agree that just because verbal abuse is not visible does not mean it cannot cause serious psychological harm. The harm it causes is reflected in the popular term used to describe the abused person—victim. It is important to look more closely at this term because the language used to describe a situation can affect how people see and respond to it. The term victim has rather unfortunate and counterproductive connotations. Victim

> "Already you have helped me by saying, 'You are a target, not a victim.' All the professional help I have received so far just says I am an accomplice or that I am a victim in a terrible situation and not much can be done. . . . I like your way of perceiving it. And believe me, after twenty-five years of verbal abuse, I really need all the help I can get!"
>
> —CELIA G.

implies that you don't have a choice. Victims are powerless and weak. They need others to help them because they can't help themselves. You are not a victim, no matter what anyone, including your friends, therapists, or parents tell you. You are not a survivor either. We prefer to use different language to describe being a partner in a verbally abusive relationship. You are a target, and you can stop being a target today. No one has to stand still for target practice. Yes, you may have been hurt by someone's anger, unhappiness, lies, accusations, and mind games. But are you a victim? No! Remove this term from your mind-set. Victims survive. Victors win. You are not going to just survive anything—you are going to win.

Ask yourself, do I want to be victimized and survive it? Or do I want to be victorious and win? If you want to win, then you are reading the right book. And fortunately, you are not alone. Many people have stopped playing the victim role, and we show you how they did it. With the information and techniques in this book, we teach you how to respect yourself and demand better treatment in your current relationship. We don't want you to leave the relationship, if you can help it, or try to change your partner. If you try that, your partner may only become more belligerent, and we have found that trying to change an abuser is an exercise in futility. We would prefer that you stay in the relationship

---

"I suffered twenty-five years of verbal and emotional abuse from my husband. I lost myself in that sick situation. I was so messed up from all the abuse, I became fragmented emotionally. He did all the classic behaviors. He alienated me from family and friends. He belittled me in front of my children. He made fun of my religious beliefs. He refused me money for nice clothes and made fun of my physical appearance. He spent what he wanted on himself. He ruined our credit. I had suicidal thoughts all the time. He punched holes in the walls, yelled, cursed, ranted and raved, and threatened to take the kids from me. He was always insanely jealous. I just endured it. My children have been scared, and needless to say, severely affected by this cycle of abuse also."

—DEE N.

---

and change *yourself* so skillfully by demanding respect that your relationship lasts.

In most cases, if you decide to leave, your life will only improve short-term.

> "I married and divorced three abusers before I realized I needed to work on MYSELF."
>
> **—DEBBIE R.**

Why is leaving often not the best choice? The reason is that there is a pattern. The same pattern of abuse will likely reappear in your next relationship because you have not yet mastered the skill of demanding respect from a partner. Unless you stop training people to abuse you, the abuse will continue. An example may clarify this pattern. Imagine a new junior partner in a law firm. Right before an important meeting, the senior partner tells her to go to Starbucks and get everyone a cup of coffee for the meeting. If she complies, then the senior partner will continue to take advantage of her and may even escalate his demands. She has just taught him that her time is not as important as everyone else's. Instead, she could respond with, "I'm sorry. I don't have time. I'm preparing for the meeting." Or, if she really wanted to teach him a lesson about her power status, she could say, "I'm busy. When you find somebody else to run the errand, make mine a Venti Mocha Cappuccino." The way she demonstrates what is acceptable treatment is in her hands. Likewise, the way you allow others to treat you is in your hands.

Our approach is not a magic relationship bullet, by any means. However, successfully addressing verbal and emotional abuse is a good start in repairing a relationship. Our major goals are to

- Show you that no one can abuse you without your consent.
- Teach you how to cease playing the victim role.
- Show you the difference between a victim who survives and a victor who wins.
- Show you how to stop abuse dead in its tracks.
- Show you why taking care of yourself ends abuse.
- Explain why you should never keep abusers' secrets.
- Give you a whole new group of friends who are also winners.
- Teach you about the Miracle Principle, which can prevent you from being abused again.

What this approach cannot do for you:

- Provide marriage counseling.
- Protect you from physical violence. If there is physical violence, get out now. Call the National Domestic Violence Hotline at 1-800-799-SAFE.
- Change your partner. (However, if you change your approach and reactions, your partner may start respecting you more and treat you better.)
- Make your partner love you.
- Give you reasons to stay or to leave.
- Agree that you are a victim, powerless, stuck, or trapped.
- Make you happy (but there's a good chance that if you master the Respect-Me Rules, you will be happier).
- Rescue you.

The Respect-Me Rule method is designed to build your understanding and skills to overcome abuse, which allows you to save the relationship, if at all possible. We would much rather you learn how to stop the abuse before starting the divorce. You must be able to identify abuse before you can address it. Targets cannot just vaguely say, "Something's not right. I'm unhappy. He must be abusing me." Targets have to be able to identify *exactly* what is abusive about the relationship, or they cannot address it properly. Verbal and emotional abuse can be so complex and cleverly disguised that it may be difficult to recognize. Here are some of the many faces of the abusive relationship:

General Disapproval

There is a pattern of anger, hostility, and criticism toward you. It can be of your looks, what you wear, your sex appeal, the way you clean house, the friends you choose, your family, the movies you like, or your faith. His disapproval is general in nature but becomes more pronounced when you have an opinion that differs from his.

You Can't Make Him Happy

You keep trying to make him happy by complying with his wishes, but the criteria changes. What you did this week to make him happy may make him angry next week. You are always caught off guard, and as a result you are unsure how to stop his anger and make a happy marriage. Nothing you do, in the long run, keeps him satisfied.

"In my relationship, what hurts me the most is that I have allowed him to control everything I do or do not do. He has told me where to work and where not to. If a man worked there, forget it. I am working in an office all by myself—boring and no fun, with no one to talk to. And he still questions and accuses me of things. It is sad, but I am reading and learning more about it so that when I do leave, I will not go back this time."

—JAMIE D.

You Walk on Eggshells

You feel as if you are walking on eggshells all the time. You never know what will set him off. Your home does not feel like a safe place because of his outbursts and criticisms. You are hesitant or even afraid to bring people home because when they leave, he will get angry about things he says you or your friends did wrong. You feel best when you are not with him because you don't have to constantly monitor your words and actions.

You Feel Micromanaged

He monitors where you go, who you see, what you talk about, and how much time you spend with your family. He may instruct you how to clean house, wash dishes, do laundry, or hang pictures. You can do very little without his oversight. He will financially control the relationship and all purchases. Even if you are expected to pay the bills and buy groceries, he will keep you on a budget, buy himself luxury items, and accuse you of not managing the money properly. If he overspends and you can't pay the bills, you, of course, will be the culprit.

He Doesn't Care What You Think

He may or may not share his thoughts and plans with you, but he definitely does not seem to care about what you think, what your plans are, or how you feel. He only asks questions about your past so he can torment you about it during arguments. You watch his programs, talk his politics, and explore his work. If you work, he only wants to know about who you work with (for possible accusations of betrayal) and couldn't care less about anything you have achieved in your field.

5

You Can't Discuss It

When you try to talk to him about problems, he gets angry and blames you, tells you that you are crazy or imagining things, gives you the cold shoulder, or says he doesn't know what you are talking about. Sometimes he listens, but he rolls his eyes or doodles when you attempt to discuss problems.

He Rewrites History

He denies saying what you heard and claims you said things you didn't. He blames you for the marriage troubles and accuses you of having evil motives against him. You believe that if you could just prove to him how much you love him and have his interests in mind, he would recognize your value and stop tormenting you.

You Can't Get Through to Him

No matter how hard you try, you cannot connect in a meaningful and lasting way. Communication in the relationship is difficult. You can't get through to your partner. Your partner's responses confuse you because your words are twisted and manipulated to put him in a superior position and make you wrong. You believe that if you could just get him to understand how you feel, things would change.

If you can identify with any of the above situations, then you are being targeted and should put a stop to it. Remember, you wouldn't tolerate this kind of behavior from a stranger. Why should you take it from

---

"I have tried with my whole soul to love her, but my honest attempts have been met with controlling and subtle verbal punishments that have—over time—made me feel small, insignificant, afraid of her wrath, and stripped of hope and dreams. My sacrifices for her are taken for granted, and I am unsure of my own thoughts and feelings, ineffective in my work, and left doubting, doubting, doubting. She cannot trust, empathize, assume personal responsibility, or apologize and seems to have no interest in personal growth and healing."

—KEN H.

---

the person you love and who claims to love you? Has someone convinced you that this is normal? One of the first things to understand is this: A good and decent person will not treat another person, especially his spouse, with disdain, hostility, or criticism. A good and decent man will treat his wife better than he treats his best buddies. And a good and decent woman will treat her husband better than her best girlfriend. A good and decent person will not hide behind scripture, culture, gender, or tradition to justify maltreatment of anyone, especially his mate.

Strangely, targets often accept the unacceptable by justifying and excusing it. Shelly kept making excuses for her husband's constant anger and criticism by saying things like

- He's trying to quit smoking.
- He just changed jobs.
- His boss is on his back.
- His mother is sick.
- His mother just died.
- His ex is trying to move his son out of state.
- I am not spiritual enough.
- I haven't proved to him how much I love him.
- If I get it right, he will stop treating me this way.

She always gave him an excuse for being mean to her, humiliating her, and discounting her. It is common for targets to spend a lot of energy rationalizing their mate's craziness away. The truth is, there are no excuses for treating someone badly, especially the one you say you love.

Chapter Highlights

- Reframe the way you think about your situation. Instead of being a victim and a survivor, you are a target and a winner.
- However unconsciously, we teach people how to treat us.
- This book is not about changing the abuser but rather learning how to change by respecting yourself.
- If at all possible, work on these abuse-stopping skills within the relationship before resorting to ending it.
- There are no excuses for treating the one you love badly.

Something to Think about

Am I ready to stop calling myself a victim—stop trying to simply sur-vive—and tell my partner to "make mine a Venti Mocha Cappuccino"?

CHAPTER 2

There Are No Victims, Only Volunteers: Understanding the Miracle Principle

No one can insult you without your consent.

—ELEANOR ROOSEVELT

AFTER LISTENING TO A PATIENT DURING a psychotherapy session carry on with a litany of complaints about her husband's mistreatment of her, Dr. Marshall asked, "Who chose him as your husband?" She fell silent and seemed perplexed. Perhaps she was expecting sympathy or a nod in agreement about how dreadful her husband was. Maybe she wanted Dr. Marshall to talk him into starting therapy and make her husband stop mistreating her. She may have even been looking for permission to leave him. Dr. Marshall offered none of those solutions. His intention was to reframe the issue in a way that required her to take personal responsibility for her situation.

One of the most difficult concepts to convey in psychotherapy is the fact that we often invite continued mistreatment from others. This is a subconscious process of which we are rarely aware. The best example of this process is a study conducted in 1981 concerning mugging victims.[1] The study's investigators came up with some surprising findings. The convicted criminals they interviewed explained they only chose to rob those who they predetermined were vulnerable through subtle body language cues. For instance, the criminals could determine how much confidence potential targets had by how they walked and carried themselves. Signs of vulnerability included moving in an uncoordinated manner and walking with an abnormal stride—taking steps that were either too long or too short. In other words, a change in walking pattern can reduce the chances of being mugged! This is but one example of how we send out subtle signals that tell others how to treat us. Those who walked confidently were telegraphing the message, "Don't tread on me."

Is it possible to send out this type of self-protective message to our partners and others with whom we interact? If so, how do we do it? That is exactly the point of this and subsequent chapters. With the right knowledge, we can acquire the power to protect ourselves from verbal and emotional abuse. And if we learn the skills to stop it early in our relationships, it is less likely to escalate into physical abuse. Of course, once physical abuse starts, everything changes. Due to the potential for serious injury, professional help is paramount, and the principles in this book should only be used with the next relationship.

"We have two beautiful children three and four years old. They are starting to feel the effects of the abuse. Also my two older ones from a previous marriage. The abuse is horrible. I want to walk away, but I am scared to death. No one understands why I stay. It is not physical. It's emotional, verbal, mental, and financial. I am willing to read and educate myself on everything I can do to protect myself. The truth is, even if I get a divorce, I will still have contact and interaction with him. We have children together. Education is the best way to help me to protect myself."

—AMANDA B.

But by stopping verbal abuse early, the likelihood of domestic discord escalating into physical violence is decreased.

The first step to stopping verbal abuse is to understand what we call the Miracle Principle, which simply states: If you don't dance together, the dance ends.[2] Other expressions also capture the essence of the Miracle Principle:

- It takes two to tango.
- If you don't get in the ring, there can't be a fight.
- If you don't take the first drink, you can't get drunk.
- If you don't like the ups and downs, don't get on the roller coaster.
- People can only walk on you if you lie down.

In other words, you have to face the fact that you are doing something that allows the abuse to continue, even if you're simply being too passive.

Patricia Evans was the first author to outline strategies specifically designed to stop abuse in her pioneering book, *The Verbally Abusive Relationship*.[3] Janet Wolitz and Melanie Beatty, in helping others understand codependency, provided the tools to find self-worth from within rather than seek worth from what a partner thinks and says. Combining these two bodies of work allows targets to learn to set boundaries with consequences. Once they understand how to use these concepts, a miracle occurs in their life. They know that they have the power to stop a pattern of abuse.

Take Off the Bull's-eye

The greatest resistance to this approach comes from those who cry, "You're blaming the victim!" One young woman, Betty, wrote to us and said, "I was too overwhelmed to do anything. I had no one. I could not help that I was not strong enough. I wanted to be. I don't believe in feeling sorry for myself, but I could not help this. Not in my eyes." Because abusers are adept at creating fear, guilt, and helplessness, it is understandable that Betty and many like her feel trapped. But *feeling* trapped is not the same as *being* trapped. Unless you are in chains, severally incapacitated, or married to a hit man who *will kill you*, you are only as trapped as you want to be. Giving you sympathy and agreeing that you are not strong enough would be the same as us stepping into the box of fear with you. What we would rather do is pull you out of that box to see your life from a new perspective.

"I felt my husband was the source of power and control in our marriage so he would have to be the source of change. I'm just now learning that all of my husband's abusive acts against me required the platform that I believe he was all powerful and I was all powerless. My husband basically brainwashed me, and I'm beginning to understand why I could never get better even with therapy as long as I was reprogrammed into feeling like I had no power to help myself or to set in place reasonable consequences for his abuse."

—SHELLEE S.

Our method empowers targets. It shows you that you *are* strong and have the power to take off that shirt with the bull's-eye on the back. Not only does it tell you that you are strong enough, but it also gives you the tools to make the necessary changes. We won't tell you that this new view of life and your role in the relationship is easy, but it is possible.

Although the idea behind the Miracle Principle is simple—we can stop being verbally and emotionally abused by not allowing it—it takes considerable knowledge, practice, and skill to implement it. The abuse-stopping techniques are introduced in the next chapter. Can they be used without professional help? We do not recommend it. Verbal abuse always has the potential to escalate into violence. Therefore, going it alone is like playing with fire. With this book, we hope to raise awareness that abuse in relationships can be stopped, especially with the proper help. Because most people are too close to their problems to see them objectively, having a professional guide is always the safest course. That is not to say that it is impossible to effectively use these strategies in a self-help format. It is simply better to get professional help. You can always ask your therapist to incorporate the Miracle Principle and the abuse-stopping strategies into your therapy if you want to use this type of approach.

Some people are lucky enough to have an innate sense of the Miracle Principle. They are virtually immune to abuse. Dr. Marshall first realized these people existed when he caught the tail end of a conversation between two college students waiting for class to begin. One was telling the other about her recent first date. She accepted because she thought he was cute and that he seemed like a nice person. However, he did a few things during the date that made her uncomfortable. For one, he talked a lot about himself—his wonderful accomplishments, his grandiose life plans—and seemed to have very little interest in knowing more about her. When she attempted to squeeze in the fact that she was an accomplished ribbon dancer, he responded with, "That's stupid." Later in the date, he yelled at her when they got lost after she had inadvertently given him incorrect directions.

Dr. Marshall heard her sum up what she thought of her date: "Can you believe this guy? I don't take that type of treatment from anyone. I feel sorry for whoever ends up with him!" It may seem obvious that no one would put up with a person like that, but unfortunately, many volunteers out there would. Instead of ending the evening quickly and saying good-bye forever, some women would have reacted differently. For instance, in response to the comment that her dancing skill was stupid, a volunteer would have frantically searched for something

> "Abusers install a mental filter in our heads a little bit at a time. Before we know it, everything we do, say, or think goes through this filter. 'Will he get upset if I do/say/think this? Will he approve/disapprove? Will he feel hurt by this?' Until we can uninstall the filter, our actions are controlled by them to some degree."
>
> **—BARBARA**

else to say that would impress him. She may have felt guilty about giving him wrong directions and become apologetic in response to his anger.

What is the difference between these two responses? Why would one woman vow never to see him again while another would take the blame? There are many possible explanations. Self-esteem is an obvious one. Someone who does not feel worthwhile does not believe she deserves to be treated well. There may also be a difference in gender role expectations. Those raised to believe in traditional gender roles could be more deferential to the man's viewpoint and accede more power to him. Or there may be differences in personality and skill. One woman may be more confident and socially skilled than another. And finally, tolerating this type of treatment may be a function of loneliness. Some women believe it is better to be mistreated than to be alone. Whatever the reason, the point is that anyone can learn to recognize the signs of abuse and make a conscious decision to stop it.

Jennifer's true story is an example of the Miracle Principle in practice. Her name and some identifying details have been changed to protect her confidentiality. Jennifer had been involved in a physically abusive relationship for many years. Eventually, she was able to muster the resources to take her two children and leave her abuser for good. She was attracted to the man in her next relationship because of his gentle nature. She felt that he would never hit her, and she was correct. However, what she didn't understand was that she had fallen into a verbal abuse trap. This was probably a result of the contrast effect. By contrast, her new love seemed wonderful because he never hit her.

Jennifer mistook his criticism as love and concern—that is, once she overlooked the harsh language. She figured he was a little rough around the edges, which was not of grave concern because there was no physical abuse involved. When she went out with her girlfriends, he would say things like, "There you go again with your cheap barhopping ways. You're a lousy mother." She would respond by calling him names also. In a way, she felt flattered that he was so jealous that he would get angry and try to discourage her from going when she planned on spending time away from him. This felt like love to her because of her previous physically abusive relationship. But she eventually sought out therapy because she felt that she and her boyfriend were arguing too much. Having come from a family in which verbal abuse was common, she had no idea that it was the major problem behind all their arguments and unhappiness.

It's about Self-Respect and Taking Responsibility

Stopping abuse means having respect for yourself and taking responsibility for how you allow people to treat you. Maybe the pattern started when you were a child and did not have the power or wisdom to stop it, but today it is different. You are not a child anymore, and you don't have to give away your power. Richard Mayer, in his book *Conflict Management,* puts it this way: "The person who experiences [abuse] must take some action. This requires taking full, personal responsibility at the moment. It requires us to acknowledge our reaction—our thoughts, assumptions, and feelings. We cannot adopt a 'victim' attitude: blame the other person and wait for some rescuer."[4]

Targets must come to the realization that the abuser cannot abuse without someone who is willing to accept their lying, berating, taunting, putting down, discounting, threatening, name-calling, yelling, and raging. Without a target, the abuse can't land anywhere. You must dance together or the dance ends. A victim, to paraphrase Mayer, is determined not by the oppressor but by the attitude of the target. Mayer said, "[Abuse] derives entirely from avoiding personal responsibility."[5] In other words, if you don't like the dance, stop dancing. It really is that simple. The reasons people keep dancing are as varied and numerous as there are partners who allow the abuse. In an abusive situation, there is often a pay-off for the victim that is very hard to see, admit to, and take responsibility for (see chapter 7).

"I believe that emotional abuse is only effective when there is an affected target. How effective is an emotional abuser without a person who feels vulnerable to abuse?"

—LYNNETTA C.

No Victims, Only Volunteers

It is hard to fathom why anyone would volunteer for abuse. In reality, abuse often creeps into relationships so slowly that it is not easily recognized at first. The target tends to excuse the abuser, thus putting on blinders. This type of rationalization is an attempt to say, "I have not made a mistake, and my future wishes and dreams with this person are still intact." We are taught to accommodate the person we love, to compromise, and do whatever else is necessary to make a relationship work. It is easy to think we are being a loving and caring spouse when in fact we are facilitating the abuse. Targets inadvertently open the floodgates to further abuse when they reward abusers' behavior by accommodating their increasing demands.

It is easy to see why targets behave this way. It is natural to expect others to behave rationally. If we treat our partners nicely by accommodating them, it makes sense that they would reciprocate and treat us the same way. Logically speaking, this should work. But it doesn't. What's so insidious about this state of affairs is that doing the logical thing when dealing with an abuser only makes the situation worse. Why is this so? Because abusers are not rational! They are so self-absorbed that being fair and reciprocating kindness does not compute with them. So what's the moral here? Recognize abuse at the outset and stop it. You cannot appease and accommodate it. It will only get worse.

This seems unfair to those who are trying to be good partners. Targets often cling to the notion, "If I could only be good enough for him, he'll finally treat me right." One of my patients recently remarked, "When I get my degree, he'll see how good I am and stop telling me I don't amount to anything and not want to cheat on me anymore." In trying to meet abusers' demands and be good enough to please them, targets volunteer for further abuse. This solves nothing. What is the solution? Learn how to stop the abuse, not how to make yourself good enough for him. You can never be good enough for an abuser to stop mistreating you, so purge this notion from your mind.

"I had been advised that if I control the way I speak, he'll love me more. I found myself speaking less, listening more, and speaking only uplifting things. But nothing happened. . . . So I shut my mouth. Shortly after I started practicing this, he became even more enraged because I could then easily detect when he was playing games with me . . . and I didn't respond. I chose to only respond when he was kind and uplifting. (Sort of following the principle . . . if you keep petting a growling dog, you will get bit.) I stopped petting the growling dog . . . and the dog became even angrier."

—BAMBI

The target's goal should be to stop focusing on how badly her spouse treats her and to ask herself, how badly will I allow myself to be treated? In other words, how low will I allow my self-esteem to be pummeled? Am I ready to set boundaries I will not allow him to cross? The greatest obstacle to ending abuse in relationships is the target's lack of knowledge about how much power she has to stop it. The Respect-Me Rules in the next chapter will help you power up that knowledge.

Chapter Highlights

- The Miracle Principle states: If you don't dance together, the dance ends.
- We are taught to accommodate the person we love, to compromise, and to do whatever else is necessary to make a relationship work. This can have the unfortunate side effect of rewarding someone for treating us badly.
- You can only be abused by someone to the degree that you allow it. You have to let him, at some level, call you names, put you down, and criticize you.

Something to Think about

In what ways have you given your abuser the power to continue? A target must give consent to be abused. She has to give away her power to the abuser and allow him to make her believe she is a victim. If you want to stop abuse and start making healthy choices, you must understand the Miracle Principle.

Notes

1. B. Grayson & M.I. Stein, "Attracting assault: Victims' nonverbal cues," *Journal of Communication* 31, no. 1 (1981): 68–75.
2. Richard J. Mayer, *Conflict Management: The Courage to Confront* (Columbus: Battelle Press, 1995), 34.
3. Patricia Evans, *The Verbally Abusive Relationship: How to Recognize It and How to Respond* (Avon: Adams Media Corporation, 1992).
4. Richard J. Mayer, *Conflict Management: The Courage to Confront.* (Columbus: Battelle Press, 1995), 33.
5. Ibid.

CHAPTER 3

Specific Strategies for Stopping Abuse: The Respect-Me Rules

If you want to be respected by others, the great thing is to respect yourself. Only by that, only by self-respect, will you compel others to respect you.

—DOSTOYEVSKY

THIS CHAPTER IS THE HEART OF our approach. It offers twelve specific rules, along with techniques to enforce those rules, that targets can use to gain back their self-respect and prevent further abuse. In the previous chapter, we learned that it takes two people for abuse to continue. Emotional abuse does not occur in a vacuum. There have to be two partners willing to engage. Here we teach the target how to *disengage* the abuser. These techniques are simple, yet effective, and can involve actions as easy as turning on a tape recorder at the first sign of verbal abuse. It's amazing how well such a simple technique can work, making the abuser self-conscious and self-censoring. Responding consistently with the right consequences to unacceptable behavior is a proven method to stop maltreatment. We call these techniques the Respect-Me Rules because they involve respecting yourself and taking responsibility for your choices. Each technique will be thoroughly discussed, with practical examples to help you put it into practice.

The Respect-Me Rules work in conjunction with setting boundaries. The purpose of setting boundaries is to protect ourselves. A *boundary* defines the limits of what treatment we are willing to accept and lets other people know what we consider unacceptable. *Consequence* refers to what we will do if that boundary is crossed. Boundaries and consequences require three steps to implement: make a choice, set the boundary, and implement the consequences if the boundary is crossed.

The Three-Part Enforcement Model

1. Pause and Choose

Choose to demand respect. Do not get defensive, mount an attack, or try to please the offender in response to his abuse. When he does something abusive, choose whether to allow it or to enforce the Respect-Me Rules.

2. Set Boundaries

Describe the specific offending behavior. For example, "I do not allow anyone to call me names." Describe your partner's specific behavior rather than attack his character. For instance, if he is abusing you with threatening body language, say, "Your fists are clenched" rather than "You're a bully." Or, "Standing in the doorway blocking my way out and shouting at me is abuse," rather than, "You are mean and scary."

3. Implement Consequences

The consequences you implement if he continues with the unacceptable behavior should be appropriate and reasonable, not to mention things you are willing to enforce. For example, you could decide that if your partner calls you a name, you will leave the house for two hours. An example of how this sequence works comes from Robert Burney's website, *Setting Personal Boundaries*. If a target chooses to set a very strict boundary she may say, "If you ever hit me, I will call the police, press charges, and leave this relationship. If you continue to threaten me, I will get a restraining order and prepare to defend myself in whatever manner is necessary."[1] A less drastic boundary-setting scenario might go like this: "If you order me to do something, I will not do it. I do not take orders from anyone. I will continue to do what I was doing while ignoring you until you treat me with respect."

The best way to set a boundary is to directly state it. You could say something such as, "If you hit the wall, throw an object, or otherwise behave aggressively during our discussion, then I will leave for three hours." You may feel like you are the one being punished and ask, "Why can't I make *him* leave the house?" But remember that we can't control others; we can only control our reaction to them. The point is to send a clear message *through action* that we have a choice of who we are with. If your partner does not treat you with respect, then you will choose not to be around him. If he starts to behave in a manner that keeps you in his company, then you have made it clear how he must treat you to achieve that out-

> "Granted, in a way, yes, I tried to change him, but I didn't do it in the sense that changing him would be the answer. I did it more like saying to him, 'If you can't be who I want, then I don't want you.' I thought that was fair."
>
> **—SANDRA P.**

come. Think about it. If your partner doesn't want to treat you right, then why would you want to be with someone like that? You may wonder what you will do for two hours if you need to leave the house due to your partner's aggression. The choices are unlimited. You can run errands, go shopping, go to a movie, get your nails done, read at the library, visit relatives, or do anything else that suits you. But here's an important consideration to keep in mind. If you are trying to save your relationship, do not cross the boundary of faithfulness by running into the arms of a potential romantic partner or doing anything else that would be considered a betrayal.

Setting boundaries and consequences serves an important function: They allow us to let go of trying to change our partners. This is very liberating because you don't have to worry about what they do! If you stay in the house as your abuser becomes hostile, you may fall into the trap of trying mightily to control his aggressive actions. It is quite a responsibility to try to stop someone's aggression. You might try arguing, ridiculing, shaming, crying, screaming, or threatening back, but these actions don't give you any control over his behavior. He is certainly exerting control over you. The good news is that you don't have to give him that control over you because you can choose how you react to him.

It is a frightening prospect to begin setting boundaries when you have been passive in the relationship. Common fears include your partner leaving you, becoming more abusive, becoming violent, falling out of love with you, or saying you are not a good partner. Unfortunately, your worst fears might come true. You must ask yourself, do I want to continue to live with the abuse, or do I want to take a risk and try to stop it? Yes, you can play it safe and continue to suffer, or you can stand up for yourself and demand to be treated with respect. The choice is yours. It is common for some die-hard abusers to leave partners who stand up for themselves. They move on to another, easier target. Do you really want to keep a partner like that?

> "I am twenty-one years old and on day eighteen of a thirty-day 'no communication break' I enforced on my fiancé. I am afraid he will decide not to marry me. I keep telling myself that the ache of being alone is better than the hysteria and fear I endured while in the abusive relationship."
>
> **—MELISSA E.**

When you start enforcing the Respect-Me Rules, your partner might accuse you of trying to manipulate or control him. This is not true. It might look like manipulation to him because he thinks, "You're telling me I can't do this." Actually, you're not telling him he can't behave badly. Instead, you are saying, "I'm not going to accept you treating *me* badly." If he wants to mistreat people, he can find someone who will allow it. You are not concentrating on what he does; you are concentrating on what you allow to happen to you. You are simply taking care of yourself by not engaging in his abuse. Allowing him to treat you this way will only escalate the maltreatment. The difference between manipulating your partner and enforcing the Respect-Me Rules is that you let go of the outcome. *He* is in control of the outcome. He can choose to respect you and keep you or abuse you and lose you.

Shelly implemented boundaries and consequences with her husband when she decided he was not allowed to bludgeon her with his anger any longer. Her boundary was, "You are no longer allowed to get angry at me or around me for any reason. When you yell, talk through gritted teeth, slam doors, destroy property, give me dirty looks, call me a name, or make any hostile accusations, I will not sleep in the bedroom with you. I will move into the bedroom downstairs for one night. If you continue, it will be two nights, and so on." He was astounded. He told her not to be silly and that she was blowing it all out of proportion. But she remained firm. Once her husband realized he could not cajole her back into the bedroom after his outbursts, the outbursts became less frequent. Shelly was as astounded as her support group members were that this simple action—telling him what he could not do to her and then enforcing consequences when he violated her boundaries—put a grinding halt to his rage.

Before we cover the Respect-Me Rules, we need to present some guidelines for using them because they represent major life changes for some people. Although the rules are simple, putting them in practice is not easy. Altering habitual behavior is very difficult and is similar to trying to quit smoking. Quitting smoking seems simple. You just don't pick up a cigarette. What makes it so hard is that every fiber of your being is screaming for another one. If you haphazardly use these rules or back down after taking a stand, it becomes much harder to enforce them. Study these guidelines thoroughly before employing the rules.

- Start with the rules you feel the most comfortable using. Enforce the other rules only after you have mastered the first set.
- Be consistent. Do not set a boundary with consequences and then not follow through. If you give in, you destroy your credibility in his eyes and train him to know that if he is persistent, you will fall back into the old pattern.
- Expect the abuse to get worse when you first enforce a new rule. Abusers will escalate their abuse to try to put you back into your place. Don't back down and don't give in! Only 100-percent consistency will get the point across and allow these rules to work.
- Remember that the abuse will not stop entirely at first, but things will get much better over time. You should notice a difference immediately. It may get worse at first because he will test your limits, but if you fail to reward his bad behavior, the laws of learning dictate that the poor behavior will diminish in frequency over time.

Consistency is crucial due to a powerful underlying psychological principle called intermittent reinforcement, or persistence training. Psychologist B.F. Skinner discovered this effect while he was conducting behavioral experiments with rats. He noticed food pellets were jamming the food chute in a Skinner box rat cage, which meant some rats were only getting a food pellet reward every once in a while for bar pressing. Normally, they got a food reward for each bar press. This intermittent reinforcement had two powerful effects on the rats' behavior. First, he noticed they were pressing the bar faster than ever to try to get the food that only occasionally came down the chute. Second, when he stopped reinforcing them altogether for pressing the bar, it took much longer for bar-pressing behavior to extinguish in the rats who received occasional rewards compared to those that consistently got a food pellet for each bar press.[2]

How does this apply to you and the Respect-Me Rules? Your abuser, the rat, finds it rewarding to abuse you because he likes the power and control, and having someone to blame absolves him of responsibility. If you're nicer to him in the hopes he will treat you better or you simply allow the abuse to continue, then he finds it reinforcing to mistreat you. Once you decide to no longer let him disrespect you by implementing the Respect-Me Rules, you take away what he finds reinforcing (remember, the rules are designed to stop providing reinforcement for abusive behavior). You want the mistreatment to extinguish just like the rat's bar-pressing. If you occasionally give in, it's the same as a rat getting intermittent food pellets. He will react by increasing the frequency of his abuse and being more persistent with it. This, in effect, renders the Respect-Me Rules and boundary-setting almost useless. It teaches him to be persistent in his abuse until you give in, which will make things worse. Do not employ the Respect-Me Rules until you are sure you can consistently enforce them. It is better not to use them at all than to use them erratically and thus incorrectly. Joining a support group before you employ the rules will be very helpful (see chapter 10).

We present the Respect-Me Rules as follows: First, the rule; second, an explanation; and last, an example of how to enforce the rule, using the three-step enforcement model outlined earlier.

The Respect-Me Rules

I. "Respect me. I deserve and demand respect."

This signifies your determination. It is a change in attitude. You now know that no one has the right to mistreat you, that you demand respect, and that you will not tolerate anything less. If you are truly convinced that you will no longer allow yourself to be a target, your demeanor will broadcast it. It will show in your voice tone, posture, and body language. You are no longer a victim. Your confidence in your self-worth will emanate from your body. Others will see it. It's not unlike the confidence that exudes from a military general, CEO, or sports star. Your abuser will notice too. It will make him vaguely uncomfortable and less confident in his approach. Soon he will come to realize what your new demeanor is all about.

As you begin to enforce the Respect-Me Rules using the three-step process, it is not necessary to communicate this whole plan to the abuser, but you should do so if you believe you have the strength.

One would think that it is common courtesy to inform your partner of your intentions in the relationship and to keep him appraised of what you are doing. Yet we understand he has not been particularly courteous to you or you wouldn't be reading this. Circumstances vary from couple to couple, and only you can decide if you should announce your intentions to change. Keep in mind that it is not necessary to explain that you are now enforcing boundaries related to your self-respect in order for these boundaries to work. In addition, if you think he will only use this to argue with you further and you are not strong enough *not to engage*, then wait before you share, if you share it at all.

If you choose to share, communicate to your partner that life has changed. You will, from this day forward, begin to respect yourself, and you expect him to respect you too. You will respond to any violation of your self-respect in a new way. One of the first responses you may get from an abuser is something along the lines of, "In order to be respected, you have to earn it." Your immediate response can be, "I agree with you. That's exactly what I intend to do."

Next, he may remind you that respect works both ways, and until you respect him, he doesn't have to respect you. This will be followed with a point or two about the ways in which you disrespect him and how disappointed he is in your lack of regard for his standards. One of many great responses is, "I am sorry you feel that way. But right now my primary responsibility is self-respect by setting the appropriate standards for myself."

Along with this announcement, say something like, "You have said some hurtful things—things I would never allow anyone else to say to me. I end up feeling bad about myself and the relationship, and I no longer want to feel bad about either." If your partner is still listening, tell him that you will communicate your boundaries and standards by letting him know what is acceptable and unacceptable treatment according to your new standards.

Your announcement can be face-to-face or by phone, text message, letter, or email, depending on your situation. It can be solely between you and him or in front of a counselor with your partner present, if you are seeing one. Should you choose not to take this step by actually communicating to your partner, we want you to write your intention down in a letter addressed to him and share it with someone. Share it with a counselor, fellow member of a support group, or best friend. Then dispose of the letter as you see fit. Your situation is unique, and you must determine how you shall lay the foundation for your new awareness of the Respect-Me Rules.

Trying to communicate with an abuser is more difficult the longer the abuse has been going on. It may be that he will disregard you, ignore you, or, if your announcement is in written form, toss it in the trash. After all, shutting down communication is part of the abuse. So such an announcement is not necessarily for your partner but rather lays the foundation for yourself. This step of stating your intentions verbally or, alternatively, writing them down, serves the very important function of rehearsal, which helps solidify your new role in your brain and will make it easier to begin implementing the Respect-Me Rules.

Three-Step Enforcement Example

A married couple is at home on the weekend.

1. Pause and Choose

The target has chosen breakfast as a good time for her husband to listen to her announcement that she will no longer tolerate abuse.

2. Set a Boundary

She tells him what her boundaries are by saying, "I deserve to be treated with respect. I will no longer allow you to be disrespectful by calling me names, smashing things on the kitchen counter, or hiding my car keys."

3. Implement a Consequence

She says to him, "There will now be consequences when you do these things. I will no longer tolerate them and allow your behavior to continue without consequence."

If he sincerely wants more details or examples, then go ahead and provide some specific examples from the Respect-Me Rules. However, if he responds with an abusive comment or action, then immediately implement the appropriate Respect-Me Rule and show him!

If he puts on a facade of not listening to you, don't be concerned. Also, do not fall into the trap of arguing with him. There is no need to argue. Actions speak louder than words! Show him. He will get the message loud and clear later on as you begin enforcing the rules.

After you take this step, either directly with your partner or indirectly with a letter you have chosen not to show him, your intention will immediately begin to equalize the balance of power. You will regain some of the strength that shifted to the abuser. This may be threatening to the abuser, and there will be resistance because you are demanding an equal amount of power. The rest of the Respect-Me Rules are designed to deal with this resistance.

2. Never defend or explain.

Never defend or justify yourself when your abuser accuses you of something. No matter what you say, he will twist, turn, misinterpret, and use your excuse or explanation to abuse you further. Don't explain your behavior, appearance, or other choices when his communication is abusive (for example, putting you down, criticizing, calling you names, yelling, humiliating you, or being sarcastic). Trying to get him to understand has not worked to improve your relationship in the past and only gives him fuel to find other ways to make you wrong. Learn to respond in ways that do not involve explaining yourself, defending your actions, or showing him your good intentions. This does not mean that you never talk to your partner, but you should only interact when he treats you with respect. If not, the conversation is over. Don't explain yourself. This prevents him from sucking you back into a defensive position.

Three-Step Enforcement Example

Raymond's girlfriend, Aggie, rips into him with, "I see you didn't take the boxes I left in the garage to Goodwill. Why can't you even do the simplest little thing that I ask? What's the matter with you?"

1. Pause and Choose

Raymond pauses and makes a choice not to explain his actions.

2. Set a Boundary

He sets the boundary by saying, "Aggie, I don't allow anyone to talk to me in that tone of voice."

"I realize that it takes two to partake in verbal abuse. One delivers, the other receives. It is a dance. I know I defend myself when I am being verbally abused. I state explicit examples to disprove the verbal attack. Unfortunately, this leads to more verbal onslaughts. I know this strategy is not working. Defending myself against the verbal attacks continues to facilitate and engage my abuser. I need to stop engaging."

—TAMMY C.

3. Implement a Consequence

Raymond walks away without answering either question or defending himself. Oftentimes, especially when targets are just beginning to enforce the Respect-Me Rules, abusers will not allow you to end the episode so easily. If Aggie continues with, "Well, aren't you going to answer me? What's the matter with you?" he can repeat, "Aggie, I don't allow anyone to talk to me in that tone of voice. I'm going home now and will return when you start talking to me in a respectful manner."

3. Do not accept or believe derogatory statements or actions.

This rule works with name-calling, criticism, put-downs, or any other situation in which you are cast in a negative light. Here is how it works.

> Him: "The dishes aren't even washed. You're too lazy to clean the house!"
> You: "I don't believe that."
> Him: "Well, I believe it. You're lazy."
> You: "You can believe anything you want, but I don't believe it."

Then resume doing what you were doing. Do not get angry, defend yourself, or engage him in any other way. This places the responsibility for accepting or rejecting the negativity with you, which is where it should be. By letting him know you don't believe his put-down and that you are not upset, there is very little possibility for the situation to escalate. You know you're not lazy, and you're letting him know that you don't believe it. He is not getting his desired reaction—to hurt you. You have defanged him. When he realizes that he cannot engage you, he has no more power over you or that situation. You have achieved your goal of setting a boundary and consequence. The boundary is that you are not willing to accept his derogatory statements, and the consequence is that you will not interact with him or give him a sense of empowerment or superiority by acting wounded when he treats you badly.

> "Just wanted to let you know I employed your stop sign tactic last night, and it worked! Thank you!"
>
> **—KELLY T.**

On the other hand, what if he calls you a name that has some truth to it, such as a fat cow? You can say, "You're right. I am overweight. But I do not believe I'm a cow." Again, you have asserted your control over what you believe and have not allowed him to control your reaction by responding with anger or hurt feelings. You do not give the disrespect any power because you don't believe it. It demotes his words to a meaningless exchange. What if a store cashier said to you, "Your hair's purple."? It's simply not true, so why would you get upset about it? The clerk clearly has a perception problem, and you don't believe that he is seeing the world correctly, so why should you get upset?

Three-Step Enforcement Example

A couple is at a party. Shania uses put-down humor when introducing her husband by saying, "Meet my husband, the 'artist.' He actually believes he can make a living off of his silly little doodles."

1. Pause and Choose

Hal pauses and makes a choice to demand respect. He does not get defensive and say, "You're always putting me down," nor does he laugh and pretend her put-down humor is okay.

2. Set a Boundary

He lets Shania know what she said was unacceptable by saying, "Yes, I do believe that, dear." He then turns toward the other couple and says, "I am a well-trained artist with talent and ambition. There are many successful artists out there, and I have the same right as everyone else to pursue my passions and talents as a career. I may even end up as the next Walt Disney."

3. Implement a Consequence

Shania's attempt at humor at Hal's expense backfired when he refused to accept or believe her negative comment. He put her in the awkward position of being overtly refuted. She gets the message that he is unafraid to publicly call her out when she violates his Respect-Me boundaries.

4. Respond with strength.

Patricia Evans suggested this rule.[3] Responding with strength means that you will start exuding your newfound strength to your partner. You let him know you are serious and will no longer be deferential to him. At times, an abusive partner can be downright mean, make wild and derogatory accusations, or order you around like a slave. A victim's response is weak and powerless: "Why are you saying such mean things? You make me feel so bad. I don't feel like you love me anymore." Since you know that you are not a victim, you don't need to act like one. Respond knowing you are worth fighting for. You can no longer afford to try to make life better for him, be good enough to earn his love, or guilt him into better behavior—all this has already taught him that mistreating you works. Now you have to unteach him, which requires you to respond with strength. Show him and yourself that you mean it by enforcing these rules.

An example of responding with strength is the stop sign technique. When your partner responds to you in an inappropriate and unacceptable way, hold up your hand like a traffic cop—palm facing your abuser—and say, "Stop! You are not allowed to talk to me that way."[4] Then resume what you were doing. When Shelly did this with her husband, she was as astounded at his reaction as he was at hers. He stopped, turned around, and walked away in confusion. She used it often at first, and his hurtful verbal attacks dropped off quickly. When he tried to "engage" her by saying, "I'll say any dang thing I want to you. You are not my mother," she did not respond or defend. The few times she regressed and tried to explain what she was doing, he sucked her right back into an argument. She soon learned the importance of Respect-Me Rule #2: *Never* defend or explain. Abusers are not rational; thus, rational explanations seldom work. If there is constant criticism, don't defend against the criticism. Just look your partner in the eye and say, "Enough. I'm not interested in your thoughts on that." Shelly got into the habit of responding to any unacceptable action with a strong, clear message that her husband could not treat her that way. And it worked!

Three-Step Enforcement Example

Georgiana's boyfriend orders her to make sandwiches for his friends who are over to watch the ball game while she is addressing thank-you cards.

1. Pause and Choose

Georgiana pauses and makes a choice not be ordered around like a maid.

2. Set a Boundary

She sets the boundary by saying, "I don't follow orders."

3. Implement a Consequence

She does not do what he ordered and continues to address her cards. If he rephrases his request with a respectful tone, she may then consider fulfilling his request and say, "Okay, give me a few minutes to finish up here." If, on the other hand, he continues to be disrespectful and says, "Stop with that respect-me crap and get me the sandwiches," she will have to increase the consequence by taking the cards, leaving the house, and addressing them at another location such as a café or the library.

5. Remove yourself if necessary.

When the situation is intolerable, you should leave as soon as possible. Situations that might warrant you leaving are if your partner does the following:

- Gets drunk and abusive.
- Gives you the silent treatment.
- Stays argumentative when you refuse to engage.
- Acts intimidating by using gestures or threatening language.
- Destroys the house or personal property.
- Hurts or scares your pet.
- Scares your kids.

Under no circumstances should you leave yourself or your children in intolerable, psychologically damaging, or demeaning situations. Always have a backup plan for a place to go when you need to leave. If you don't plan to be away overnight, you can nurture yourself by going to a movie, getting a spa treatment, or going window shopping. If you plan to be gone overnight, you can stay with a relative or friend, go camping with the kids, or stay at a hotel.

Three-Step Enforcement Example

Crystal and Tom arrive at their home. Their dog, Bruno, who was alone all day, chewed a hole in the pillow. Tom, in a fit of rage, picks the dog up and tosses him against the wall.

"My boyfriend is trying to convince me not only that what is going on is not verbal abuse, but that I am abusive for leaving when things get bad. I don't know. I'm so mixed up right now about the whole thing. It helps to know I've got support out there from people like you."

—KARMA J.

1. Pause and choose

Crystal pauses and makes a choice not to respond to rage with rage.

2. Set a Boundary

She sets her boundary by not allowing Tom to hurt their dog. She says, "We don't abuse animals in this house."

3. Implement a Consequence

Crystal takes her dog and leaves the house for the night. She says, "Because you hurt the dog, I am leaving for the night. If you do it again, I will report the abuse to the ASPCA."

6. Use repetition.

This technique ensures you will be heard and get a response. This is a great technique from assertiveness training. Just keep repeating yourself until you get an answer. Do not allow your spouse to turn it around on you by accusing you of something else or change the subject so you get lost in another argument. Here are some situations where the use of repetition is appropriate:

Silent Treatment

When your partner is trying to punish you by giving you the silent treatment, discontinue everything you normally do to meet his needs, such as fixing dinner or gassing up the car. Whenever he inquires about your "negligence" by asking something such as, "Where's my shirt?" simply repeat your original request until the topic is addressed in a civil manner. Do not resume meeting his needs until you are satisfied. Do not tell him where his shirt is until he responds to your issue. He may turn it into a power struggle, and it may take weeks to resolve, but just keep repeating.

For instance, Sarah normally washed her husband's work clothes and had dinner on the table for him every night when he got home from work at six o'clock. She noticed that the atmosphere in the home was becoming increasingly hostile and tense. He was snapping at her a lot and finding fault with many little things. He finally exploded one day when he found out she had bought a Christmas toy for their daughter that he considered too expensive. He responded by punishing her with his silence and refusing to talk. He had promised to get the car inspection sticker but did not out of passive aggression to go along with his silent treatment. At this point, a real need was not being met, which is not acceptable in a fair and balanced relationship. When the deadline for renewing the registration passed, Sarah stopped fixing his dinner. He said, "Where's my dinner?" She responded in a reasonable and neutral voice, "As soon as I have the inspection sticker so I can renew our car registration, I'll have your dinner on the table." It was not easy for Sarah to remain cool and disengaged and not defend herself with a retort such as, "Why should I cook you dinner when you won't get the car inspected?" He tried to re-engage her by saying, "Oh, so this is the kind of game you want to play. Don't you think it's kind of childish?" But she did not fall into the trap of defending herself. He said, "I'll get it done next week." That was fine with Sarah. She wanted to watch the evening news instead of fixing dinner for him for the next week anyway.

Misunderstanding You

When a partner deliberately "misunderstands" what you said, repeat the original statement. Do not explain why you are repeating it and do not rephrase it. If you do, the abuse is prolonged with continuing word games. When you know your partner knows what you mean but purposefully misunderstands what you say, don't use your energy except to stop it. Repetition is one approach. If he persists in "misunderstanding" what you are talking about, say, "Okay," and end that conversation. Shelly successfully used this a number of times with her ex-husband. Often within fifteen or twenty minutes, he would poke his head in her office, where she went when ending conversations with him, and say, "Oh, did you mean. . . ?" He did understand her. The real motive was to exert power by forcing her to ask the question or state things in a prescribed manner. Here's an example:

Before Using Repetition

You: "How did it go with the dogs today?"

He: "What?"

You: "You know. The appointment."

He: "What are you talking about?"

You: "When you took the dogs to the vet to get their rabies shots."

He: "Why didn't you say that in the first place? If you would speak more clearly, people might know what you are talking about once in a while."

Using Repetition

You: "How did it go with the dogs today?"

He: "What?"

You: "How did it go with the dogs today?"

He: "What are you talking about?"

You: "How did it go with the dogs today?"

He: "I don't understand what you are asking."

Then you reply, "Okay," and walk away. After a while, he is likely to come back and say, "Oh, you mean with the dogs' rabies shots?" By keeping control of the situation with repetition, you have not given him an opportunity to belittle you and have avoided falling into his "you must say it exactly right" trap.

Roadblocking

This occurs when the abuser changes the subject by diverting you or accusing you of something else (throwing up a verbal roadblock) so he doesn't have to address your concern. He doesn't want to respond, so he changes the focus of the conversation.

Let's give an example of a man who is trying to reform his marriage and is addressing a recalcitrant, abusive wife. A typical concern of the husband might be, "I don't like it when you spank the kids. We need to discuss alternate ways to discipline." She responds, "Look who's talking! If you hadn't called me names all those years, maybe I wouldn't be so stressed with the kids all the time."

You can't defend or respond. Look the abuser in the eye. Repeat

"At 3 a.m. he rolled on my hand after surgery. I tried to move away, but he woke up and said I was ungrateful and I was trying to get away from him. I went in the other room. He followed and turned on the overhead light and began yelling and cussing. My son had a friend over, so I went outside and he followed, still yelling. I hid in the bathroom until he found me, and he said, 'Give me a kiss so I can go spend the day with my brother.' HELP!"

—MAGGIE

the statement. Request that your partner look at you and repeat the question, ignoring the attempts at verbal roadblocks. Repeat your request until he addresses your concern. Eventually, the abuser will realize that diversions no longer work, and he will begin to respond to your concerns.

Three-Step Enforcement Example

Michael wants to know if his wife, Tanya, has paid the Internet bill because the browser will not respond. He does not know that she spent the money getting a new tattoo. Instead of answering the question, she goes on the offense and accuses him of not making enough money to pay all their bills.

1. Pause and Choose

Michael pauses and makes a choice to not get pulled off track by getting angry or apologetic.

2. Set a Boundary

He has set the boundary that he deserves a simple answer to a direct question. He asks her to look at him and repeats the question.

3. Implement a Consequence

He repeats the question until she answers it, regardless of what else she says. This stops Tanya's roadblocking. She is no longer controlling the situation, and he is not responding to her abusive accusation.

7. Do not reward nasty and negative behavior.

The best kept secret in emotionally abusive relationships is that we train people how to treat us. If we jump when they yell, we have taught them that yelling works well with us. If we meet their demands when they act mean, we teach them that being mean to us works—they get what they want. Often we try to placate our mates when they get hostile. We engage in extra niceties to convince them we love them and didn't mean to make them angry. But if you get nicer when they get meaner, what does that teach them? It teaches them that being mean brings them rewards. Instead, when they treat you badly, you should immediately draw upon the three-step enforcement procedure that will stop it. Do not walk on eggshells. Do not do more for them. And do not comply with unreasonable demands. Instead, withdraw your support or helpfulness and only offer it back when they treat you with respect (see chapter 6 for an in-depth explanation).

Typically an abuser unrelentingly criticizes the way a target does things. The target tries to please the abuser and stop the criticism by "correcting" her so-called deficiencies to the satisfaction of the abuser. This may seem harmless, but giving in to a rude approach preludes a proliferation of criticism because as you change in response to the abuser's need to feel powerful, you reward him. The abuser will never be satisfied because it's not really about how you're doing things; it's about his control. You can never be good enough to stop the nasty behavior, so don't try. One of the best ways to understand this concept is to ask yourself how trying to please him has worked so far.

Three-Step Enforcement Example

Becky is washing windows with paper towels. Leonard snaps, "That's a stupid way to clean windows." He then condescendingly explains that the "proper" way to wash windows is with a squeegee so that Becky won't waste paper towels and leave lint all over the glass.

1. Pause and Choose

Becky pauses and makes a choice not to reward his nastiness.

2. Set a Boundary

She sets the boundary that she can make her own decisions about how to carry out her housecleaning chores.

3. Implement a Consequence

Becky calmly tells Leonard, "Here. If you have a better way to clean the windows, be my guest." She hands him the bottle of cleaner and then goes about another task. Her actions throw cold water on his attempt to gain power at her expense.

8. Do not keep his secrets.

Do not be afraid to tell those you trust about the abuse. Everyone needs a support system. We have learned that we are only as sick as our secrets. Emotional abuse should not be hidden any more than violence should. It is healthier for both partners to have everything out in the open. Those who employ this strategy will soon find there is little abuse left that needs to be exposed. However, when these abuse-stopping strategies are first employed, everyone within reason should be told what is going on. It's like smoking. The more people you tell that you are quitting, the harder it will be to start up again. The more people you tell about your abuse, the harder it will be for you to allow the cycle of abuse to continue. Here is a Catholic analysis on why it is merciful to tell.

> The verbal harassment also damages the verbal abuser. Interestingly enough, Catholic teaching views wrong or evil acts as being even more damaging to the perpetrator than to the victim because the agent of a bad act is damaging his own moral nature and character (see Catechism of the Catholic Church, 1731, on the effect of our free acts). The victim is not making himself a bad person—he is suffering as an innocent party, just as Christ did. The verbal abuser, on the other hand, is making himself into a worse person every time he launches an attack on another's person, reputation, or life work. So to draw attention to the problem is a favor to the verbal abuser because the exposure will make it harder to sustain. In the language of the Church, drawing his attention to the problem is an act of mercy.[5]

Be prepared for your abuser to say you are betraying him and the relationship, that you are blowing things out of proportion, that you are lying, and so on. In other words, he will likely verbally abuse you for

"I am probably the oddball email for you. You see, I am not the target of abuse. My wife is. I am the one who has been dishing it out. Yes, I believe I did abuse because I could, and it got me my way."

—RICH H.

"telling" about the verbal abuse. Tell anyway, because exposure is one of the most powerful social forces for correcting wrong behavior. The only reason Tiger Woods was able to get away with cheating on his wife (a type of emotional abuse) for years with more than a dozen mistresses was that nobody told. The minute his secret was exposed, everything changed dramatically. Now, all of a sudden, Tiger's main focus is to be a better father, husband, and person. If someone had not revealed his secrets, Tiger's priority would still be playing around on the back nine. Secrets keep relationships sick.

John Prin, author of *Secret Keeping: Overcoming Hidden Habits and Addictions*, has informative articles on his website regarding secrets and why you should not keep them. He writes, "Keeping secrets can make us neurotic. Secrets can be so toxic that a person is driven to self-destructive and insane acts. Then come the addictions, the violence, the lying and alibis . . . even suicide."[6]

Three-Step Enforcement Example:

Lisa is socially isolated by her husband, Jerry. She found out that he has been having phone sex when she saw the three-hundred-dollar charge on their credit card statement. When Lisa confronts Jerry, he says to her, "We're a family unit now, and what goes on in this family stays in this family. You shouldn't talk to your sister or mother about what goes on here because that would be a betrayal of our sacred trust."

1. Pause and Choose

Lisa pauses and makes a choice to not keep his disrespectful secrets.

2. Set a Boundary

She lets Jerry know his behavior is disrespectful to her and unhealthy for their relationship, and she is not going to live in a relationship with unhealthy sexual secrets.

3. Implement a Consequence

Lisa will not only tell her sister and mother, but she will also tell their marriage counselor. Future consequences will be that she will tell their pastor too unless Jerry starts to respect her by ceasing his phone sex.

This rule regarding telling is so important that we have devoted an entire chapter to it (see chapter 8).

9. Record everything.

This is a great abuse-stopping technique. Shelly used it with her abusive ex-husband to great advantage. She started writing everything down because her husband so often rewrote history between them. He "forgot" what he said or did, minimized his destructive behavior, accused her of saying or doing things she didn't, and generally made her feel crazy. He drove her to the point that she was not sure what was happening. In counseling, he told the therapist that it was sad that she felt it necessary to write everything down to prove herself. The counselor said it was a great idea and asked her to record each argument or incident right when it happened (this was before she learned the above techniques, which stopped the arguing altogether) and then to give a notebook to her husband and ask him to record his recollection of what went on. The therapist wanted them to see how differently they viewed things, which would provide an opportunity to compare and communicate. Shelly wrote in a journal and asked her husband to do the same with their next three fights. When she handed him her renditions so they could do their assignment, he tore the pages up and threw them in the trash. This demonstrated very clearly that he wasn't interested in communication—just belittling her.

But the great thing was, Shelly found that he couldn't rewrite history anymore. Before using the journaling technique, she was unable to tell him the exact words he used or the day and time it occurred. When he claimed, "I never said I wouldn't give you the ten thousand dollars I owe you and you'd have to sue me for it," she could pull out her journal and set the record straight. It was very empowering. All he could do at that point was to call her a liar, yet they both knew that she wasn't because the journal had recorded the facts. Don't let your partner get away with denying, forgetting, or rewriting history—just start using a journal to keep the record straight. This can also be used as invaluable evidence for your divorce attorney should the relationship dissolve.

Keeping a journal does not mean you have to write on a pad of paper—you can use the computer or record events with a small device, even your cell phone or iPod. A word of caution—anything you use can and probably will be discovered by your partner. The problem is not that they know you are recording, in fact, it's probably best that they know (see Respect-Me Rule #10). The problem is that they may destroy it. So take precautions and get back-ups (digital for recordings and hard copies for text journals) that are put in a secure location.

Three-Step Enforcement Example

Marie is mopping the kitchen floor and accidentally knocks over the garbage can. The noise wakes up Frank, who flies out in a rage, accusing Marie of not allowing him to get his needed sleep. An argument ensues and Marie reminds Frank that he wakes her up regularly for minor issues that could easily wait until the next day. He accuses her of making up tales, saying that he always respects other people's sleep.

1. Pause and Choose

Marie pauses and makes a choice to not accept Frank's rewrite of history and his accusations that she was making things up.

2. Set a Boundary

Marie pulls out her journal and says, "It's not acceptable to accuse me of making things up and rewriting history between us."

3. Implement a Consequence

Marie reads from her journal the dates, times, and circumstances of all the times he has woken her up frivolously. She adds, "If you try to rewrite our history again, I will post my journal on my support group website along with your distortions because you are not allowed to question my sanity."

10. Call attention to verbal abuse.

It is important to immediately let the abuser know when verbal abuse occurs. This powerful psychological technique allows the abuser to self-monitor. Consider, for example, an overeater who habitually and unconsciously grabs a bag of chips to munch on when watching TV. Simple awareness of how destructive this habit is, such as keeping a food log, is a good motivator for change. The overeater can then take corrective action such as not buying chips, eating lower calorie snacks, or consciously deciding to eat an apple instead. Even if your partner has not agreed to work on making the relationship better, he may respond when you call attention to the obvious abuse.

An ingenious way to call attention without saying a word is pulling out a recording device. Recording his words prevents him from rewriting history (see Respect-Me Rule #9). More importantly, if he thinks you are recording the incident, he is less likely to be abusive because this evidence will make him very self-conscious. Thus you benefit in three ways: you have a voice journal, you have made him conscious of abuse without saying anything, and he is less likely to be abusive. Shelly began using this method on her husband. When he stormed into her office, she would whip out a small recorder and click it on. Most of the time it did not even have tape in it, but his behavior changed dramatically because he became conscious of what he was doing.

Don't misconstrue calling attention to what they are doing as license to play amateur psychologist, for example by explaining your partner's underlying motives for the abuse. This will only infuriate him and escalate the abuse. Simply point out to him that you perceive abuse to be present. In some cases this will be enough to stop him, particularly if he is motivated to work with you to improve the relationship by taking responsibility for his actions. Pointing out what you consider to be abusive is intended to work along with the other Respect-Me Rules. For example, say, "Criticizing the way I fold laundry is something I consider abusive. Stop it." If he doesn't stop, say, "Since you don't approve of the way I fold laundry, you can fold your own." Then place his clothes in a basket on his bed or in his closet.

Often you only have to point out the abuse, especially if there is no particular consequence you want to enforce. Letting your partner know you are aware is enough—but never let him continue. If he continues the behavior, you must enforce a consequence. He may continue his antagonism by striking back even more strongly, but this should only be temporary. Eventually, calling attention to abuse in conjunction with the other techniques will make him more self-conscious and, under normal circumstances, the abuse will diminish. For instance, if a discussion turns heated and your offender begins yelling, you could simply say, "You're yelling and it scares me." Just being aware of what one is doing tends to act as a powerful psychological brake. Other examples are:

- He says, "You lazy slob." You reply, "Name calling is abusive."
- He is ignoring you and giving you the silent treatment. You say, "Giving the silent treatment to a partner is considered abusive in a relationship." If awareness alone has no effect, employ a consequence: "I am taking myself to the movies."

- He fails to give you a Christmas gift. You state, "Failing to recognize a special occasion is a type of emotional abuse."

Three-Step Enforcement Example

Graciela's spouse, Manuel, fails to acknowledge her academic achievement of graduating from college. Manuel does not say anything, attend the graduation, give her a graduation gift, or even take her out to dinner to celebrate her achievement.

1. Pause and Choose

Graciela pauses and makes a choice to not suffer in silence and take on the role of the victim.

2. Set a Boundary

She lets Manuel know that failing to acknowledge her major academic achievement is considered emotional abuse because it diminishes her.

3. Implement a Consequence

Graciela tells Manuel, "It is unacceptable not to celebrate my achievement. Are you aware that ignoring my achievements makes me think that you don't care about me? It's not a requirement to take me out to dinner, but if you don't, I will go out to dinner and celebrate my achievement with my girlfriends."

II. Use a prompt.

An example of a prompt would be a button with the words "Respect Me" pinned to your shirt. This is a constant reminder that things have changed. Your abuser will see it every time he looks at you. It's another way of stating, "I have power." Be ready for a negative reaction from him when he first sees it. He may make a snide comment like, "Respect? Yeah, right. I'll give you respect when you earn it!" An appropriate response might be to just smile and say, "We'll see about that." If your abuser is more entrenched in his need to have power over you, he may be even meaner and say, "Nobody could respect a woman like you." How do you respond? Again, do not defend or explain yourself, unless he asks about it in a respectful way. If he truly wants to know what the button is, you can tell him what you are doing in a forthright, sincere manner. Otherwise, if he snidely asks, "What is *that*?" the conversation is ended. Go right into the other Respect-Me Rules by saying something like, "I don't allow anyone to speak to me in that manner. I'm going out. I'll be back later." You may want to read appendix A for some great "prompt" slogans you can use.

Three-Step Enforcement Example

Joe has a long history of criticizing Rhonda when he gets home from work and chastising her for things such as not starting the dishwasher, not putting the asparagus in the proper refrigerator drawer, or leaving a toy in the driveway. She finally has enough of his criticism and decides to put a plaque up in the kitchen that says, "Rule #1: Rhonda never deserves to be criticized. Rule #2: When you think Rhonda did something wrong, see Rule #1." When Joe gets home from work, he fails to see the humor in the plaque, smashes it, and tells her to clean up the mess.

1. Pause and Choose

Rhonda pauses and makes a choice not to let Joe intimidate her or discourage her use of a public prompt about how she deserves to be treated.

2. Set a Boundary

Rhonda says to Joe, "It is not acceptable to destroy my property."

3. Implement a Consequence

Rhonda leaves Joe's mess on the floor for him to clean up. She takes money out of the family budget to replace the plaque and creates a screen saver on the computer that ticker tapes the same message.

12. Be a model of respectful behavior.

The natural tendency when someone makes a cutting remark is to blast them back. Here is an example:

> He: "Is that a double chin, or are you just staring at me over a pile of pancakes?"
> She: "Where did they baptize you, at Sea World?"

Although most verbal abuse is more crude than put-down humor, the principle is the same: like begets like. If you want to teach your partner to treat you with respect, then it is counterproductive to treat him disrespectfully. You cannot react with name-calling or whining about how badly he treats you. Mature reactions are sometimes hard, especially when you get so angry and frustrated that you just want to retaliate for all the hurt created. You want to dish a little back or feel sorry for yourself and lick your wounds. But both responses allow the perpetrator to justify his behavior. Acting maturely helps your partner see how childish he is acting. Although payback can feel emotionally satisfying, it will backfire in the long run by inviting more abuse. Object lessons don't work. An abuser won't see how much his negative remarks hurt you. He will just use what you said as ammunition to step up his attacks with the attitude, "Look at what she did to me. She deserves it!"

Why does he abuse you? The simple answer is because he can. But there are also many underlying reasons that he began the abuse. One of them is likely to be dysfunctional family background consisting of copious arguing, bickering, verbal abuse, or worse. In other words, he had poor role models of family relations. He learned how to interact with others in a dysfunctional manner. When stressed, he will tend to revert to what feels comfortable and familiar. His responses are habitual and automatic. If you react to his abuse at the same level, it will simply serve to perpetuate more of the same. However, by not climbing into the ring with him to duke it out blow by blow, he will be left stranded.

Eric Berne formulated a nifty counseling technique called transactional analysis, which explains how our adult patterns of interaction stem from childhood experiences in our families. This creates a "life script" in which we continually replay childhood patterns even though they may be dysfunctional in adulthood. Berne says we are always in one of three ego states—parent, adult, or child—when interacting with someone else.[7] We won't go over the whole theory here, but we will use one example that illustrates the Respect-Me Rule at hand. If someone is calling us names, we can react to him from the child ego state by name-calling back or whining about how badly he treats us. Berne points out that it is much more productive to instead react from the adult ego state. Here is an example.

Abuser: "You fat cow!"
Target: "That comment is out of line. If you're upset with something, we can discuss it."

Here the target respectfully refused to put her gloves on and get into the ring to fight. Furthermore, she took the high road, which makes her abuser look immature and crude by any objective standards. And finally, by reacting from the adult ego state, she has invited him into the ring of maturity and respectful problem solving. He may even start imitating the better relationship skills whether he is aware of it or not.

Remember the Miracle Principle: If you don't dance together, the dance ends. The positive role-modeling technique is another way to disengage from abuse. You might say it's the inverse of the following: "If I invite him to dance respectfully with me, he just might take me up on it." So, as hard as it is, do not let him suck you down to his level. Stay on the high road. At a minimum, you will feel better about yourself due to your exemplary behavior, and you will not be providing him with more justification for abuse.

Three-Step Enforcement Example

Jenna and Mark are at a company party. Jenna is extremely jealous because she saw Mark talking to another woman. She storms over to Mark and pours her drink over his head while screaming, "You just find it so hard to spend time with your wife when there's a cute tramp around!"

1. Pause and Choose

Mark pauses and makes a choice to maintain his dignity.

2. Set a Boundary

Mark lets Jenna know her behavior is childish and unacceptable by saying, "Sally, I'd like you to meet my wife, Jenna. Although she may think you're a tramp, I don't. I hope this does not put a damper on the five-million-dollar advertising contract your firm has with my company."

3. Implement a Consequence

Mark later tells Jenna, "You will not be invited to attend the next company party. If you disrespect me again at the party after that, I will not go to a party with you for six months."

Conclusion

None of these Respect-Me Rules need to be discussed with your partner in order for them to work because they are not so much about him as they are about you and what you allow. How will you allow others to treat you? Is it okay for a neighbor to call you fat, flabby, stupid, or selfish? If it's not okay for a neighbor to do it, it's not all right for your partner to do it. Ask yourself, if the owner of the laundromat criticized you on the soap you use, the way you separate your whites and colors, or the fact that you use hot water and not cold, and if she considered you beneath her because of your "stupid" choices, how would you react? Or, imagine yourself at a park with your child and another mother is there with her toddler. She observes you and offers comments about the way you should interact with your child. She lets you know you don't dress your child right—the sweater isn't warm enough, or you should put a hat on your child in this breeze. She criticizes how you talk to your child and instructs you on how to discipline him because she feels you are lacking the correct knowledge. For how long would you take this?

Chapter Highlights

- The Respect-Me Rules are abuse-stopping techniques that targets can use to disengage the abuser.
- The superior response to abuse is to take an active, purposeful, and planned role in stopping it rather than a naive, passive, and ineffective response, such as arguing back, which only serves to perpetuate the abuse.
- The Respect-Me Rules will stop you from providing reinforcement for your partner's abuse. However, you must be consistent in using them. Giving in will train him to persist in his old ways because he feels that it is only a matter of time until he can break you down and get you back under his control.

Something to Think about

You cannot fix the problem until you change your mind-set. Do the Respect-Me Rules provide you with a new mind-set? How is it different from what you were doing in the past? Can you identify and list a few of your past mistakes that have allowed him to perpetuate the abuse?

It is important that the target be aware when abuse is occurring in order to know when to pull out the appropriate abuse-stopping technique from her bag of tools. You will find out how to recognize various forms of abuse in the next two chapters.

Notes

1. Robert Burney, "Setting Personal Boundaries—protecting self." *Joy2MeU*, accessed September 12, 2009, http://www.joy2meu.com/ Personal_Boundaries.htm.

2. C. B. Fester and B. F. Skinner, "Schedules of Reinforcement." *American Psychologist* (1957).

3. Patricia Evans, *The Verbally Abusive Relationship: How to Recognize it and How to Respond.* (Avon: Adams Media Corporation, 1992), 133.

4. Ibid., 141.

5. Oswald Sobrino, J. D., M. A., "A Good Resolution: No More Verbal Abuse." *Catholic Analysis,* accessed January 1, 2005, http://catholic analysis.blogspot.com/2005/01/good-resolution-no-more-verbal-abuse.html.

6. John Prin, "Confessions of a Liberated Secret Keeper." *John Prinn Articles*, accessed January 30, 2010, http://www.johnprin.com/articles/ art-confessions.htm. Appeared in *The Phoenix*, (St. Paul, June 2001).

7. Eric Berne, "A Summary of Transactional Analysis Key Ideas." *The International Transactional Analysis Association,* accessed January 2010, http://www.itaa-net.org/ta/keyideas.htm.

CHAPTER 4

More about Abuse

Abuse in the home is not a rare problem, it is just rarely admitted as one.

—HIDDENHURT.CO.UK

THE AUTHORS DECIDED TO DEVOTE a whole chapter to what causes your partner to be abusive, not because it makes a difference in how you respond to his abuse, but because most people just want to understand the nature of what they are involved in. Knowing what causes him to mistreat you does not necessarily provide the tools to fix it. In fact, it can make things worse because once you find a label that fits your abuser, you will be tempted to learn all you can about that type of abuser and stop focusing on what really makes a difference—your responses.

Domestic abuse is the general term used to describe any type of non-violent abuse by family members or intimate partners such as a spouse, ex-spouse, boyfriend, girlfriend, ex-boyfriend, or ex-girlfriend. *Domestic violence* and *domestic assault* are the terms used when violence occurs. Other terms used for domestic abuse include:

- Intimate partner abuse
- Mental cruelty
- Emotional abuse
- Verbal abuse

Abuse is multifaceted and complex and involves both words and gestures—the tone of voice, the look in the eye, and knowing how to intimidate the target. According to the Woman's Health Library, the

"It took me a while to recognize what was happening to my relationship with my wife when I got frustrated and angry when talking with her. I kept chasing down the 'lack of respect' path and was never able to 'earn' her respect. As a successful working professional supporting the family both financially and as a father, I feel humiliated by the poor attitude from my wife."

—BRUCE C.

abusive person is usually male, and women are often the target.[1] However, domestic abuse also occurs against males. Although we most often hear about men abusing women, there are also serious problems with the reverse—women abusing men—and abuse occurring in a number of other non-traditional relationships, such as same-sex relationships. Just for simplicity's sake, we will generally use the traditional abusive scenario of the male abusing the female. This in no way minimizes or fails to recognize any other gender combination of abuse. This book is simply about stopping abuse in its tracks and enforcing the Respect-Me Rules, which apply to any type of couple.

Let's define some terms so it will be clear what we are talking about. Domestic abuse is complex and requires some sorting out to make clear. Below is a partial list of the various types of domestic abuse. These terms can help you understand what is happening in your situation. It is important to know what type of abuse is occurring in order to make a decision about the appropriate response for enforcing your rules. You need to know that abuse *is* occurring in order to implement the responses offered in this book. However, it will not be productive to use this list to identify what is wrong with your partner so you can focus on fixing him. This list is meant for you to recognize abuse so you can learn how to respond in the optimal way without trying to fix him. Nothing in this book is about fixing others. It is about you and what you allow in your life. It's not why do they do it; it's why do you allow it.

Types of Domestic Abuse

Note: You can ask yourself the questions that appear in this section to help you recognize if your partner is engaging in that type of abuse.

I. Physical Abuse

Physical abuse includes hitting, slapping, pulling hair, pushing, choking, restraining, kicking, using weapons, throwing things, pressing or forcing sexual intercourse, and engaging in unwelcome rough sex.

Warning: We put violence at the top of the list because of the high potential of physical harm, up to and including death. Physical abuse is almost always preceded by verbal and emotional abuse. Although one precedes the other, violence crosses the safety line when you no longer can predict or effectively deal with the abuser. When dealing with verbal and emotional abuse, you shouldn't have to worry about your safety as you train the abuser to respect you. Once that safety line has been crossed, however, change needs to be implemented *outside* of the violent relationship. The safest response to violence is to remove yourself to a safe place. If your partner has crossed the line into actual physical violence, we ask you not to use the Respect-Me Rules approach with him but instead seek immediate professional guidance and support.

2. Intimidation

Intimidation includes frightening someone by harsh looks, gestures, or actions; smashing things; punching walls; destroying personal property; harming pets; and displaying weapons.

Does your partner have a pattern of

- Slamming doors, punching walls, hitting or smashing objects, and scaring you?
- Kicking or in any other way mistreating your pet?
- Taking out a weapon in a clear attempt to scare you?

"Because my husband dominated and controlled just about everything in our marital relationship, I lost focus on myself. Everything was about him, so naturally when I first endeavored to learn about domestic abuse, all my attention went to why HE was like this and what caused HIM to behave like that. I think nurturers who end up being targets of abuse are especially prone to this dynamic of losing sight of ourselves as we shift the focus away from ourselves and onto how to help our abusers."

—SHELLEE S.

- Destroying your property when displeased with you, such as ripping your clothes or swiping the dinner off the table with his arm and then telling you to clean up the mess?
- Driving recklessly when unhappy or angry at you? Are you afraid to say anything because you know it will only get worse?
- Trapping you in a room and daring you to argue or disagree with him?

3. Isolation

Isolation includes keeping someone from going where she chooses; not allowing someone to go to school, work, or other people's homes; listening to phone conversations; opening her mail; following her around; persistent questioning of her whereabouts; and limiting transportation. Isolating a partner can escalate to trapping her, refusing to let her leave, restraining her, and locking her in a space to control her. Some experts consider this physical violence, and it is one of the borderline behaviors between abuse and violence. If your partner's attempts to isolate you include physical restraint and locking you up, you need to seek professional help because he is close to crossing the safety line into violence. Isolating a person involves taking away autonomy, freedom of choice, and independence. In fact, it is designed to create a dependency on the abuser.

Does your partner have a pattern of

> "My son-in-law doesn't allow my daughter to come to any of her family events or even to visit with any of us. When she calls us, he is in the background listening to everything that is said. He calls her numerous times when she happens to be away from where he is 'to make sure she is okay,' even though I have personally heard him say, 'Where are you and what are you doing?' when she was at the grocery store on her way home from work!"
>
> **—DANNI F.**

- Discouraging you from contact with family and friends?
- Insisting on accompanying you whenever you leave the house?
- Calling you constantly or insisting that you call him so he can monitor your whereabouts?
- Taking away car privileges or having only one vehicle that is preempted by him?

The above examples are considered forms of isolation and should not be tolerated. And yes, there are ways to stop it.

4. Emotional and Pyschological Abuse

Emotional and psychological abuse include being jealous, making accusations, judging, making put-down jokes, lying, manipulating, embarrassing, creating a hostile atmosphere, playing mind games, rewriting history, withholding sex, substituting pornography for intimate relations, blaming, and making the target feel guilty or humiliated. Emotional abuse is differentiated from verbal abuse in that it diminishes you and makes you feel bad without using demeaning or angry words aimed in a direct verbal attack. Here are a few additional facts about emotional abuse based on the work of Virginians Against Domestic Violence.[2]

Emotional abuse

- is often disguised as a way of "teaching you to be a better person."
- may have longer-lasting effects than physical abuse.
- often leads to poor health, especially sleep disturbances.
- adversely affects the children of the abused.
- often starts out so subtly that the target may adapt and allow the abuse to continue without realizing it, even though at some level she suspects something is wrong.

Does your partner have a pattern of

- Making you mistrust your memory because his version of events differs so much from what you recall?

"We argued one night about primary and secondary colors and I, an artist with a diploma in visual art, said that in painting the primaries are blue, yellow, and red. Because he was taught about the primaries in light, which is different, and he insisted that what I knew was wrong. He puts down my beliefs, calls me gullible, etc. If he doesn't hear what I say or remember what I have said, he will insist that I didn't say it and that I am imagining things. This occurs all the time. It is driving me mad."

—TERRI W.

"I have been in an abusive relationship for two years now. Thank you for words of power. They inspire me when I feel so weak for not getting out of this. He enjoys tormenting me and calling me names. This is so sick. I want my self-esteem back, and I want to regain the confidence that I had before I met him."

—HEIDI E.

•Accusing you of having affairs and monitoring your email and voicemail to the point that you are afraid to communicate with anybody?

•Making you feel that you are always wrong and everything is your fault?

•Putting a negative spin on innocent situations? (For example, if you ask, "Would you like me to fix you some eggs and toast?" he barks, "Why didn't you say 'good morning'?" in an accusing tone.)

- Allowing his needs to take priority over yours?
- Counting his opinion and not yours?
- Telling you that you do not know what you are talking about?
- Ignoring your input because he feels it's not important?

The above examples are considered forms of emotional abuse and should not be tolerated. And yes, there are ways to stop it.

5. Verbal Abuse

Verbal abuse includes name-calling, insults, sarcasm, shouts, and threats.

Does your partner have a pattern of

- Calling you names such as pig, witch, idiot, or crybaby?
- Referring to you in derogatory terms such as fat, stupid, ugly, ditzy, or lazy?
- Raising his voice to win an argument or control you?
- Making snide, sarcastic remarks?

Abusers may try to make excuses by saying, "I lost control," but verbal abuse is really a way for them to gain control. Verbal abuse should not be tolerated, and yes, there are ways to stop it.

6. Minimizing, Denying, and Discounting

This type of abuse includes making light of the abuse, saying it did not happen, denying responsibility for what happened, and rationalizing why the abuse occurred. For example, your partner may scream in rage and later claim he has a right to be angry and that he mustn't hold it inside. He minimizes or denies the effect it has on you. You can't work on a problem together that your partner denies or hardly recognizes.

Does your partner have a pattern of

- Saying that you exaggerate the severity of your arguments?
- Claiming that he wasn't yelling, and in fact, you were the one who was screaming?
- Congratulating himself for letting things roll off his back, saying you make the conflict worse because you won't let go?
- Saying you watch too much Dr. Phil and things would be fine if you didn't listen to all those quacks?

The above examples are considered forms of minimizing and discounting and do not need to be tolerated. And yes, there are ways to stop it.

7. Using Children

Using children includes threatening the children if the partner does not do what the abuser says, making the partner feel guilty about the children, alienating affection, and threatening to take the children away. Children often become pawns to outmaneuver the target. They are used and manipulated for the strategic benefit of the abuser, and their needs are trampled. This is especially cruel for the children because they don't want to be caught between parents; they just want unconditional love. Abusers are willing to hurt their own children just to gain an advantage over their partner.

Does your partner have a pattern of

- Arguing in front of the kids and making you look bad so the kids will side with him?
- Telling the kids that they can't go to the amusement park because their mother blew the money on an expensive coat?
- Telling the kids bad things about you in private, saying you have mental problems and are not stable?
- Threatening to take the kids away from you if you don't behave?

Using your kids as pawns is a terrible form of abuse, and it doesn't need to continue. Yes, there are ways to stop it.

8. Male Privilege

Male privilege occurs when a man treats his partner like a servant, acts like the master of the castle, makes all the important decisions, believes he's always right, defines his partner's role, and invokes religious doctrine with which his partner does not agree.

Does your partner have a pattern of

- Reminding you that the man is the head of the household?
- Telling you that a woman must be obedient to the man?
- Saying that men are more logical and are better able to make good decisions?
- Reminding you that his training or experience makes him the expert?
- Believing he is always right?
- Insisting that you and the children must practice his religion when you prefer to practice another one of your own choosing?

Male privilege is abuse, and it doesn't need to continue. Yes, there are ways to stop it.

9. Economic and Financial Abuse

Economic and financial abuse includes preventing the spouse from working outside the home, making her ask for money, and not letting her know about the family income.

Does your partner have a pattern of

- Saying that a woman's place is in the home?
- Refusing to let you participate in purchase decisions?

"Most men think they are always right. It is the way they are, so is it still abuse? My psychologist thinks I should point out to my boyfriend that this is abusive, but I know that he will just disagree or say that I am too sensitive. I am looking for the door instead."

—TERRI W.

"My husband is gaslighting me on our finances. He will do things like hide my car keys from me for several days and then put them back, claiming they were there all along. He will then use the incident like the car keys and say I am too senile to handle our finances, so he makes all the decisions, just like you have listed in your examples of economic abuse. I am a psychologist."

—DR. C.L.

- Handling all the family finances and never revealing the records?
- Giving you a spending allowance without your input on the budget?
- Buying whatever he wants yet making you justify your purchases?
- Making all the financial decisions for the family without your input?

Keeping you ignorant of family finances is a form of abuse, and it doesn't need to continue. Yes, there are ways to stop it.

10. Coercion and Threats

Coercion and threats include threatening to harm a partner, her family, or her friends; report her to welfare; destroy her property; or commit suicide. An abuser may force the target to drop criminal charges, do something she does not want to do, or do something illegal.

Does your partner have a pattern of

- Saying, "You don't want to know what I will do"?
- Saying, "If you leave me, I will take everything and leave you penniless"?
- Threatening divorce?
- Saying, "Don't make me do it!"?
- Threatening to break things or hide your valuables until you give in?

Coercion and threats are a form of abuse, and it doesn't need to continue. Yes, there are ways to put a stop to it.

Awareness of domestic abuse is a relatively recent cultural phenomenon. Attitudes and behaviors that are easily recognized as unacceptable, immoral, humiliating, and even illegal in society are often tolerated at home. The recognition that women are not chattel owned by their husbands is relatively recent. In the past, society tolerated women being treated as less than and subservient to their husbands. As a result, many women have allowed themselves to be treated badly and may have been told by parents, religious doctrine, and society's subtle messages that this is the way to be feminine and nurturing. Women have also been told that if they are "good enough," they can get men to treat them well. They have accepted behavior from their partners that they would not tolerate from anyone else. In the past, we did not have a name for the way men mistreated women. Now we recognize it as domestic abuse. This raising of consciousness now gives women the insight and skills required to demand an equal amount of power and respect.

Chapter Highlights

- Understanding domestic abuse should not change the focus from adjusting your own actions to trying to fix the abuser.
- Domestic abuse is not limited to a male abusing a female. Females can also abuse males, and abuse can occur in same-gender relationships.
- The ten types of abuse rarely occur alone. Abuse is complex, and the different types of abuse are often intertwined and occur simultaneously.

Something to Think about

Abuse is about one person's control over the other. If you use your understanding of these concepts to try to change your partner's behavior, you are guilty of trying to control him. Healthy control involves controlling *your* reactions to him and enforcing *your* boundaries and limits.

Notes

1. UAB Medicine, UAB Health System. *Woman's Health Library*. Section on Domestic Violence, accessed September 25, 2010, http://www1.uabhealth.org/UAB_WH/P06791.
2. "Emotional Abuse Hurts," *Virginians Against Domestic Violence*, Online Brochure, Copyright 2005, accessed July 3, 2007, http://www.vadv.org/Resources/emotionalabusehurts.html.

CHAPTER 5
Abuse Patterns and Cycles

Each time you take a spin on the cycle of abuse you lose a little piece of yourself.

—HEART2HEART.CA

YOU NEED TO UNDERSTAND THE CYCLE of abuse in order to put a stop to it. Otherwise the cycle will likely continue, particularly because it has a reinforcement component, which tends to perpetuate it. When you understand how the abusive pattern ensnares you and where you are in the cycle, it will be easier to employ the abuse-stopping strategies presented in chapter 3. During courtship, no doubt your partner was charming, attentive, and seemingly everything you wanted. Abusers can keep up this original charm for only a short time, even though it is long enough to snare you. Once you are committed to the abuser, things begin to deteriorate ever so slowly, which makes the change nearly imperceptible, particularly given that you are likely to adapt to the maltreatment. This sets up two different realities—yours and his.

The two different realities may look like this: From your perspective, you believe that if you can love him enough, be good enough, and please him enough, then you can make him happy. He won't treat you badly, and the result will be a good relationship. From his perspective, he is irritated that you can't seem to get things right. He may believe that you are being purposely uncompromising, aren't trying hard enough, or do not understand the importance of what he wants you to do. When you don't do things "right," he steps up his demands by escalating his approach. He starts showing his displeasure while trying a variety of behaviors to find which work to control you and keep you in your place. He may start out by raising his voice. When that doesn't satisfy him, he will attempt other methods such as shouts, name-calling, sarcasm, put-downs, and threats.

Seldom do his compliance-enforcing behaviors show respect or concern for you. The actual underlying psychological dynamic at play is that he is unknowingly making you a target for his own sense of inadequacy. Even if you do everything requested of you, it will never satisfy the abuser because he is really project-

> "I gave up control of my life because of my husband's insistence that he should be in charge, and then everything would be all right. That has not worked out. His anger only got worse, although he has gotten control of his road rage (after several tickets). He did take over my business, which we had to close this year, so now he is in total control of the family income. I need to take back control of my life; I am just not sure how."
>
> **—LEE E.**

ing his own insecurities and inadequacies onto you. Until he addresses his own deficiencies, nothing you can do will ever make him feel whole. This is why we say it is a fruitless approach for you as the target to try to work on him. That's his job. Remember, no one can force him to examine and fix his own issues. He may never have the insight or the willingness to do so. Therefore, the only promising course of action for targets is to work on what they *can* control, which is what they are willing to put up with.

In chapter 4, we learned what the different types of abuse look like. In this chapter, we will examine the cycles of abuse in a relationship from the abuser's point of view and from the target's. If you understand the dynamics of the cycle of abuse, you will begin to understand how his perception of events and yours (which will be quite different) sabotage your ability to stop his maltreatment.

From his perspective, and the way many professionals explain it, there are three main stages in the cycle of abuse: the building of tension, the abuse event, and the honeymoon. The patterns found in each of these stages, as felt by the target, is as follows:

Stage 1: The Building of Tension
- The atmosphere thickens.
- You have a vague feeling of discomfort.

- You begin to feel as if you have to walk on eggshells.
- You worry you will do the wrong thing and set him off.
- He becomes more irritable.
- The complaints start.
- You can tell by his body language that frustration and anger are building inside of him.
- You know what's coming.

Stage 2: The Abuse Event

- He finally loses control and lets you have it with name-calling, put-downs, sarcasm, and so forth.
- He feels relieved and in charge of the situation, and you are most likely emotionally devastated.

Stage 3: The Honeymoon

- The abuser feels pangs of guilt and remorse.
- He brings you a bouquet of flowers to make up with you.
- He tells you he really loves you and did not mean to do it.
- He promises it will never happen again.
- He acts especially loving toward you and bathes you with attention. Sometimes it is a sincere response, but it can also be a manipulation in reaction to you leaving and his desire to bring you back.
- He minimizes the event or blames it on outside sources (alcohol, his job, stress, or you).
- You are hoping against hope that he really means it this time. After all, your relationship and future happiness depend on it.

Here's a vignette from Shelly's abusive relationship that illustrates the above cycle of abuse:

> Little things would set him off, and I never knew what it would be. Maybe the dogs barked and woke him up and it was my fault, he missed an appointment and it was my fault, or I closed the door to the bedroom and the latch clicked, and I was accused of doing it on purpose to disturb him. I wanted to be a good wife, and so I tried harder. "Pick your battles," I told myself. No one incident was any big deal, so it wasn't worth fighting about, but the pattern escalated and his anger increased. The tension was building to where he would be intensely critical of me, and no matter what I did, I couldn't please him.

Then the abuse would go into full swing. He would go on a rampage—breaking things, slamming doors, and name-calling. He broke dishes, phones, and TV remotes. He once tore the dashboard off my truck as I was driving. He would sweep everything off the counters and pull things out of the cupboards. My house would be littered with broken glass, broken mementos, and an enraged man who looked like he wanted to rip my face off.

After all of this chaos, he would then inevitably enter into his remorse stage. He was *so* sorry and promised never to do it again but qualified it with something like, "You should not have provoked me." His more notorious way of diverting responsibility was to say, "I hate it when I do this because now you are focused on my outburst and not the real issue." The real issue to him, in his distorted perception, was always something I had done wrong to make him act that way. I would be so relieved that his rampage was over that I desperately clung to the hope that I could satisfy him and he would not do it anymore. I can't believe I let this cycle repeat itself over and over for so many years without fully understanding its power over me.

Every target knows how this insanity progresses. After the honeymoon stage, the process begins again and keeps repeating. The target wants help and seeks out resources such as friends, parents, books, and support groups. People who want to help often offer traditional tidbits such as, "It's not your fault. You're a victim and a survivor. You're not alone. There are court-ordered anger management programs that a judge can force him into. Take him to couple's counseling." All of these comments are helpful and might offer temporary relief. But the biggest drawback is that the target maintains the focus on the abuser and the relationship rather than honing in on what can make the biggest difference—the choices she makes.

At this point, many targets mistakenly believe we are blaming them. They cannot understand why we can't see how bad their partner is. "Don't you understand what he's doing to me?" But let's look at this another way. Rather than looking at it only through the lens of the traditional cycle of abuse, let's build a new view. Yes, the three-phase cycle does occur, but it is only part of the picture. These stages mainly capture *his* perception, but what about what *you* are going through? Your reality can be more complex than what is going on with him. You are actually going through a grief cycle in your struggle to cope with the situation. His cycle is limited to venting and blaming. There is no real attempt at a solution. It's too easy to repeatedly vent and get relief.

However, for you, there is much more to it. You are mightily trying to fix things. You are attempting to transition from a broken relationship to a healthy one, and you keep getting trapped in his cycle. If you understand the true agent of change,

> "After the breakup of my relationship with Clay, I found myself mourning the loss of him in my life. When I discovered this, I wondered what possible reason could cause this reaction. What finally came to me was that I wasn't mourning the loss of Clay at all. I was mourning the loss of the romance I had in the beginning of the relationship and the loss of what might have been with him, and that's all. Once I understood this, all the feelings of needing to mourn magically went away."
>
> **—LEAH S.**

you will short circuit the cycle by stepping out of the line of his target practice. We know this is hard to do, especially when your partner is "making up to you" and apologizing. He is *so* nice and promises never to do it again. It keeps you trapped by a thread of hope that things will finally improve. However, the flaw in hoping is that nothing will change unless one of you starts doing things differently. Your relationship will not flourish simply because you both love each other and are soul mates. It is often hard to believe that it won't get better because after the abuse incident has occurred, the abuser is usually tender and sweet, convincing you it won't happen again. And if he's a skilled manipulator, he will convince you that somehow you caused him to behave abusively. You may end up apologizing to him while you're cleaning up his mess after he smashed your wedding china all over the kitchen!

At some point, most targets get angry when they finally realize that they've allowed their abusers to repeat the cycle of abuse. There's plenty of anger to go around—at your partner for hurting and deceiving you and possibly at yourself for allowing it to continue for so long. Anger is an understandable part of human nature and is one of the transitions that you must experience as you work through the stages in your cycle. It can give you the energy you need to work toward change and emerge as a winner. However, it can be toxic if you get stuck in that stage.

Every transition in life requires going through stages, not unlike a baby learning to walk by first sitting up and then crawling and finally walking. The transition from victim to target to winner requires that you work through *your* stages and learn how they differ from *his*.

Your cycle is similar to Kubler-Ross's stages of grief[1] because you are grieving the loss of your dream relationship. You once felt love, hope, and promise for your partner. You thought you had found your soul mate, but then abuse took your dream away. You need to grieve the loss of your fantasy.

As previously explained, the traditional cycle of abuse consisting of built tension, an abuse event, and the culmination of the honeymoon phase primarily describes the abuser's cycle. The cycle we show here describes the target's mind-set of grieving when abuse spoils her dreams of the perfect relationship. An adaptation of Kubler-Ross's stages of grief to a target's perspective of the abuse cycle looks like this:

Stage 1: Denial, Isolation, Self-Blame

At first, you tend to deny that any real abuse is taking place. You are usually in shock and mentally pull away from the truth for as long as you can. You make excuses for your partner's behavior, withdraw from your usual social contacts, and blame yourself for causing the abuse or for not being good enough to avert it.

Stage 2: Anger

Once you admit that real abuse is occurring, you may be furious at the person who inflicted the pain or at others for letting it happen. You are often angry with yourself for picking the wrong partner, even though he seemed wonderful during courtship. You may decide to leave the relationship, fester in your anger as a victim, or retaliate in a fit of anger.

Stage 3: Blame the Perpetrator

At this stage, you denigrate the one who hurt you and find fault with everything he did. It feels good to vent, but unfortunately it also fuels your anger. You see yourself as a victim and a survivor, powerless to stop the forces that drove the perpetrator to victimize you. You feel justified in all your angry reactions. If you are afraid of your abuser, you have fantasies of him dying or of you getting even, but you seldom voice those thoughts, even to a therapist. If he could only get the right treatment, you tell yourself, things would be okay.

Stage 4: Depression

Once the anger and blame dissipate, you start to feel numb, although anger and sadness may be buried deep underneath the surface. You feel powerless once again and begin to feel hopeless. You make excuses about why it is best to forgive and forget in order to continue the relationship. You hope things will improve and that the abuser will change if you are good enough. You begin to regret all the actions you took in anger and feel guilty about your fantasies of getting back at him. Your depression may become so severe that you withdraw and give up. There is no more zest in life. You feel trapped.

Stage 5: Acquiescence or Action

When the above emotions have run their course, you face a crossroads. One choice is to acquiesce to your partner and make reconciliation during the honeymoon stage, with only perfunctory hopes of change. (For example, he promises to get help, or you vow to stop doing the things that trigger him.) If you concentrate on the perpetrator changing, which most of us initially do, progress will be prolonged and painful. If, while at the crossroads, you choose to acquiesce, then the cycle begins anew.

Alternatively, you can choose to make effective changes in yourself by joining a support group or learning the Respect-Me Rules, for example. If you implement and enforce these changes, progress will soon be evident and, as a bonus, the abuser may benefit as well. Positive action will eventually help you reclaim your life.

Initially, the abuser's cycle is long in duration, but your grief cycle transitions quickly and is often complete within an hour. The first time he mistreats you, your anger may be fleeting because you can't believe what just happened. Blaming him and feeling bad are also of short duration because these feelings are supplanted with your quick acquiescence since he is likely, early on in the relationship, to quickly enter his reconciliation stage to please you. While you are in the acquiescence stage, he is in the reconciliation stage, and the relationship is in the honeymoon stage of the abuse cycle.

As the relationship slowly accommodates and adapts to the abuse, the cycle stretches into days. As the abuse continues, the cycle lengthens to weeks or months of withdrawal, not talking, depression, and harboring anger. You can see how the abuse cycle is toxic and erodes the relationship. However, there is hope. By understanding the dynamics of abuse cycles and how the stages in your cycle differ from his, you can begin to effect positive change.

Chapter Highlights

- The traditional model of the abuse cycle focuses on his reality. Your reality involves grieving the loss of the ideal relationship and is more complicated than his.
- Once you recognize that you are living in an abusive relationship, you can do something about it by choosing to act when you hit the crossroads of acquiescence and action.
- If you're stuck in one of the grief stages, such as being angry that he never changes or feeling depressed and hopeless, your feelings are preventing you from transitioning to the last stage, where you can break the cycle by taking action and stop being his target.

Something to Think about

You can't change your partner because you don't have the power or the right. We live in a democracy. He can do whatever he chooses. There is only one person you can change, and that is you. You will be able to stop being a target for his abusive behavior, but he has to be the one to decide to have a change of heart.

Note

1. Elizabeth Kubler-Ross, *On Death and Dying* (New York: Touchstone, 1997).

CHAPTER 6

How Did I Get Myself into This Fix?

Not to know is bad; not to wish to know is worse.

—NIGERIAN PROVERB

IT'S HUMAN NATURE TO ANALYZE the situation when things go wrong in a relationship and try to fix the situation by fixing your partner. In order to learn how to stop being a target, you cannot look at the abuser and determine why he became so callous to your needs. Why? Because you already know that you can't change him. You don't need to know why he abuses. You need to know why you allow it.

In this chapter, you will learn about the codependent attitudes and behaviors that make targets accept the unacceptable. Codependency cripples people and interferes with solving the abuse problem. Codependent behavior is a very complicated topic in its entirety, but for abuse it simply means, as Dr. Charles Whitfield defines it, "the loss of self to others."[1] For a target of abuse, it means that the abuser takes center stage. The target defers everything to the abuser by giving up her self-respect and self-esteem. She tries to earn his love by

> "Someone in our support group said that she drove herself nuts trying to understand WHY he couldn't see/admit what he had done to the marriage. Boy did I identify with that. Finally she realized the only important *why* was why she allowed herself to be treated so badly for so long. Boy did I need to hear THAT."
>
> **—BARBARA C.**

allowing his needs to trump hers. And as a backlash, she often tries to "fix" his callous ways rather than fix herself.

In the support group Al-Anon, they say relatives try to control the drinking habits of the alcoholic. Likewise, in ACOA (Adult Children of Alcoholics) groups they say the children try to control the alcoholic parent. And finally, with abuse, a target tries to control the abuser. At first you may not see how you try to control your abuser. After all, abuse is about control, and he is obviously trying to control you! An example from Shelly's life illustrates this:

> Realizing my husband was likely verbally abusing me, I spoke to my sponsor in a 12-step program. I explained that my husband told me how to wash the dishes, when to put the clothes in the dryer, at what temperature I was allowed to open the windows, and what lights I was allowed to use and when. During an argument, my husband shouted, "Stop trying to control me!"
>
> Laughing, I said to my sponsor, "Can you believe he accused *me* of trying to control *him*?"
>
> She paused and said in a low voice, "But, Shelly, you *are* trying to control him." I was shocked! What was she saying? My sponsor went on to explain that I was trying to control how he felt and what he thought about me. I wanted him to think differently, act differently, and feel differently, and my behaviors were an attempt to change how he felt about me.
>
> It was a moment of clarity. Yes, my husband *was* trying to control me, but his control was overt and mine was covert. I was trying to earn his respect and love by being the best wife ever, the best stepmother to his son, and so good and spiritual that he would stop his anger out of gratitude for my sacrifice. Wow! I *was* trying to control him. It was time to face my demons. It was imperative to discover how I came to be this covertly controlling person who was willing to allow myself to be overtly controlled and abused, all the while claiming victimization at the hands of this mean, selfish person. Why did I accept this outlandish treatment?

Any target who decides she wants to get better eventually asks the same question. How does a loving, well-meaning, logical adult become codependent on abuse? How does she allow someone to treat her with disdain?

There are three main ways:

1. *She is reliving trauma.* This is where she seems to attract abusers like a magnet because she was raised in such a way that she has come to expect and is comfortable with unacceptable treatment.

2. *Her culture or family background trained her to adapt to abuse.* This often occurs with women who once had respect for themselves but don't recognize they have fallen for an abuser. The partner changes the relationship dynamics so slowly that the target adapts and is barely aware that abuse is occurring.

3. *She teaches her partner to abuse her.* When she tries so hard to be "good," she teaches him that being bad works. The target may marry someone who had little inclination to abuse and slowly teach him that when he abuses, he gets what he wants. Invariably, the abuse increases.

Reliving Trauma

Reliving trauma is a force most people are not aware of and exerts an insidious influence on those who are seemingly victimized. It occurs when those who have been victimized early in life subconsciously seek out similar situations throughout their lives. An example would be a woman who was sexually abused as a child. How might this affect her adult choices? She may, unfortunately, choose to work in a profession, such as prostitution, where she continues to be victimized, objectified, and exploited by men. If asked what she thinks of men, she would likely respond with deep-felt hostility for them, complaining that they all are no good, that they mistreat women, and that they cheat on their wives. Isn't this a strange situation? Logically, one would expect that someone who was victimized by men would choose to avoid them or at least try to stay out of harm's way. Instead, she chose the opposite. She put herself in a situation where men were able to exploit and possibly hurt her.

> "I am a widow in a relationship with a man that fits so many of the criteria of emotional abuse that I have been reading about. I'm educated and had a wonderful relationship with my husband, so I'm stunned to find myself in this position."
>
> **—AMBER R.**

How can this seemingly irrational behavior be explained? The concept of reliving the trauma serves a number of psychological functions. First, the subconscious mind is drawn to what it knows. This is also the reason the child of an alcoholic has a higher risk of entering into a relationship with an alcoholic partner. Second, there is an unconscious need to correct the original problem. When these two psychological needs are put together, we can see recurring self-destructive behavioral patterns.

Imagine a little girl growing up with an alcoholic father. He defines the nature of men for her as she develops. She wants his love desperately and struggles to obtain it. Usually, it is in a very distorted fashion. She may have to take on the mother's role to compensate for his poor functioning in the hope of gaining his love. As an adolescent, she is now primed to feel the same type of emotional attraction to a similarly impaired man. She hopes that if she loves and cares for him and puts forth enough effort, she can "fix" him and receive what she needed emotionally from her father as a child but was never able to obtain. The subconscious dream of achieving this ultimate victory over past injustices is the psychological equivalent of the Holy Grail. Now is her chance to finally meet this frozen need. But if we strip away her subconscious, wishful thinking of finally taking control and getting the satisfaction of

---

"This is information I need. I also use other self-help material to allow me to deal with my past. I was an incest victim and had abuse issues all the way into the relationship with a man for twenty years. I could never do anything right, was fat, and all the other crap. I thought it was me and not him. I am learning now about relationship dynamics and have no desire to be in any relationship until I work on my issues. Women are taught that their worth comes from having a successful relationship with a man. I am reading *The Dance of Wounded Souls*. The author is a codependency counselor. He does not blame women but says they are set up from early childhood programming to be in these types of relationships—societal beliefs about romantic relationships."

—ANDREA G.

---

finally making it right, we will find that she is merely reliving the trauma—assuming, of course, that she fails to reform her significant other, which is most often the case.

Is there scientific support for this interpretation of events? One line of evidence comes from the work of Dr. Jackie White, a professor of psychology at the University of North Carolina in Greensboro. She compared the backgrounds of young women who were raped on campus with those who were not sexually victimized. She found that the raped women were more likely to have a history of sexual victimization.[2] Does this make sense? Wouldn't a woman who had been raped not take any chances in the future? Wouldn't she protect herself by being extra careful and avoiding all vulnerable situations? Yes, that's logical, but it is not what happens, according to the study. The raped women seemed to be using much poorer judgment by placing themselves back in harm's way!

Of course, getting raped was not her fault. A man who chooses to rape a woman is completely to blame and should be held accountable with criminal prosecution. However, everyone would agree that a woman who chooses to enter a dorm room containing five young men who are drinking late at night is far more likely to end up being raped than a woman who passes on the invitation out of caution. This is what those who are not reliving any type of earlier trauma typically choose to do.

Unfortunately, many targets fall into this category and attach themselves to people with whom they can play out their previous traumatic scenarios and try to make right something that went terribly wrong in the past. Abusers may be doing the same thing. Each is trying desperately to fix things while entrapped in reliving the trauma. The target's only way out is to recognize what is happening and refuse to engage any longer, set limits, and enforce them.

> "I can't change whatever happened to you as a child that may have influenced the way you are now behaving—and you can't change it either. The important thing to realize is that you are not a child anymore. You are now an adult, and you have the chance to choose what you think, feel, and do."
>
> **—DR. PHIL**

Culture and Family Background

As little girls, we are told to be nice—we're made of sugar and spice. If we're good, our Prince Charming will come along, and life will be grand. We're set up to believe that if we get it right and have the right words, behavior, look, dinner, reaction, response, lifestyle, tone of voice, gesture, resource, and counselor, then we can create a happy marriage. It is ingrained in us that the only thing necessary is to be pure of heart in order to bring out the best in the beasts and frogs. Unfortunately, this belief doesn't require us to take control of our world and enforce Respect-Me Rules, only that we be good and sweet and kind, with the expectation that we will be rewarded with a prince. Learning to be passive sets us up for both adapting to abuse and teaching our abuser that abuse works.

> "Much of this abuse acceptance occurs without the codependent individual feeling abused! More accurately, these individuals do not feel OK enough to expect respectful treatment at all times, and to notice when it is not forthcoming."
>
> **—DR. IRENE**

Adapting to Abuse

Even if you didn't get the "pure in heart" message as a child, you can still slip into codependent behaviors because of the process of adaptation. Many men and women develop codependent behaviors around abuse. For example, the abuser may begin by saying, "Oh, are you going to wear that dress?" The next time he might say, "Don't wear that thing. It's too revealing." It progresses to, "You're wearing too much makeup" and then to, "Your thighs are too big," "Makeup makes you look cheap," and, "You're too fat." This may progress so slowly that the target has adapted over time, trying to correct what her partner saw as imperfections. Because she became accustomed to hearing these put-downs and because they began as mild observations, she does not respond with the outrage that would have occurred if he had started out with, "I don't want to be seen in public with Miss Piggy."

Because abuse begins slowly and we adapt to it over time, it is difficult to recognize. We get so used to it that it doesn't seem abusive but rather a normal part of the relationship. In addition, some religious messages, fairy tales, and our desires to be good and compliant wives and mothers prepare us to accept the unacceptable. An abuser begins to find fault and criticize, and a person who has accepted the "pure of heart" message is sure she can earn the love and respect of her partner. All she must do is get the right combination of words and behaviors that can somehow create a happy relationship. You may have inadvertently developed this pattern by believing the following:

- If you can just say the right thing, he will "get it" and stop hurting you.
- If you can convince him how much you love him, he will appreciate you.
- If you do what he wants, you will stop triggering his anger.
- If you could just get it right and meet his needs, he will love you again like he used to.
- If you find the right article, counselor, or program for him, things will get better.
- You do most of the giving in the relationship, and he does most of the taking.

All of these are considered codependent behaviors and thoughts. If you didn't start out codependent (many targets don't), your reactions of trying to please and placate the abuser often lead to codependency.

Teaching the Partner that Abuse Works

Targets often ask, "Why doesn't it matter to him when I tell him how much it hurts?" Because your reality is not his. He probably has little or no idea what he is doing or how it affects you. Or if he does, that is just the reaction he wanted. But more than this, and in all likelihood, you have actually taught your partner that his abuse works. The first time that you scramble to meet his needs when he yells, you teach him that when he yells, you scramble. If he gives you a look of disapproval and you immediately pull back and shut up, he learns that giving you "that look" works. It would be a very unusual person indeed who wasn't tempted to use behaviors that they see work when they want to get their way. Do you identify with any of the following codependent behaviors?

- When he is irritated, you try extra hard to understand what he wants so that you won't make the same mistake again.
- When he accuses you of deliberately trying to upset him or deliberately "forgetting" what he said, you usually apologize

and promise not to do it again, even if you don't think you did it deliberately.

- When he tells you not to do something, like visit your mom even if you really want to, you try to see his side and do not do it because you don't want to make him feel angry or hurt.

- When he instructs you on how to do a chore, you usually do it his way because it's not as important to you as it is to him.

- When he yells at you, you do what he wants because you don't want him to get angrier.

- He has certain things he likes you to wear or not wear. You believe if you comply, he will treat you better about other things. Besides, it shows he cares.

- If he calls you a name, you usually try to figure out how you can make it up to him so he won't call you that again.

- When he orders you to do something, you do it. If you ask him to say "please," he belittles you, so you just do it. It's no big deal.

- When he is really unhappy with you, you try very hard to figure out what you can do to get back in his good graces.

- You believe that if you can show him how much you love him and want to please him, even in the face of his anger and disapproval, he will begin to trust you and treat you better.

It is really sad to realize that any of the above actually creates the very thing you were trying to avoid. It is similar to B.F. Skinner's rat that receives pellets if it presses the bar. The abuser presses the bar (yells, gives a look, demands, orders, berates) and you give him a food pellet (comply in response to his abuse).[3] Ask yourself what you have just taught him.

The good news is, if you have taught your partner that it is okay to treat you disrespectfully, you can unteach him. He will likely begin to learn when you put boundaries in place and stop supporting his pathology at every turn. At this point, your abuser will have two choices— either learn or lose you. We hope that you will let him lose you before you lose yourself.

Codependent Behavior Makes Abusers Worse

As we prepared this section of the book, a powerful example of how society prepares women to accept abuse aired on a talk radio program.

"This was truly amazing! I hadn't realized how I had let every kind of abuse creep into my twenty-year marriage. I see now that it's me allowing these things to continue and that the more I show him my love, the more I'm giving my blessing to this increasingly cruel nonsense! No more. Thank you so much for helping me see beyond the 'episodes.' I have a long way to go . . . but I feel FREE already!"

—JOHANNA

How fortuitous. The advice came from a popular relationship talk show host. Let's call this the case of the transformed man. The caller, a young wife in her early twenties, asked, "How do I get my husband to stop being sarcastic with me?" The host asked for an example, and the young woman said, "When my husband gets home, he'll say something sarcastic like, 'The sink is full of dishes' or 'The house is so cluttered.'"

"Well, is it?" asked the host.

"Yes, but I have the baby and . . ."

"Then it's not sarcastic, is it?" snapped the host. "It's just a statement of fact. Why don't you see that your work is done, and you will transform your husband."

The young mother tried to explain her situation with a new baby but was cut off again. She finally agreed to the host's advice in a discouraged voice. The relationship guru explained how it was the wife's responsibility to transform her husband by not picking on him for stating the facts but rather to passively comply with his demands, stop whining, and supposedly transform the man into a gentle and unsarcastic being.

What happened here? This relationship guru just indoctrinated that young mother with a slew of complete falsehoods:

- Her perceptions were not reality (even though the young mother heard sarcasm in her husband's voice, she was told he was not sarcastic—he was just being factual).
- She was not a good wife (she was told not to complain about him when it was her behavior that should be in question).
- Her behavior was the cause of her husband's words (the message was that if she had a clean house, he would not have to point things out to her).

- She could transform him (if she were subservient, he would be transformed into a Prince Charming).
- She was the one responsible for a happy husband and good marriage. (This was the underlying message of the whole dialogue. Where was his responsibility to be understanding, helpful, and respectful?)

This guru failed to realize that if the young woman followed that advice, she would transform her husband, all right—into a sarcastic, abusing bully. He was already on that path. I sincerely hope that the young mother did not try to stop the sarcasm by rewarding her husband when he disrespected her. Unfortunately, this abuse-perpetuating message is all too common.

You see, your codependent behavior *does* work to change the abuser's behaviors but not in the way you want. It reinforces the bad behavior you want to be rid of. In fact, nothing you do to appease an offender will make a happy marriage or loving relationship. Appeasement does, however, let the abuser know that if he treats you badly, he gets what he wants. He usually twists all your attempts to get him to stop treating you badly and makes you appear to be the culprit. He will always win, as explained in Patricia Evans' *Controlling People* (a must-read for any target).[4] Even though he will always win when you try to change *him*, *you*, on the other hand, will always win when you focus on changing *your* responses and set and enforce *your* boundaries.

Caring is wonderful. Helping, when asked in a respectful way, is nice too. However, "helping" by attempting to change him will not be appreciated and certainly will not get the results you want. Caring for, nurturing, and compromising with your loved one is a beautiful expectation in a healthy relationship. But do not confuse those things with accepting responsibility for your partner's happiness and accepting abusive behavior to make your relationship better.

You may not have begun as a codependent in your current relationship. But if you allow yourself to be mistreated in an ongoing pattern in order to stay in the relationship, by definition, you are codependent now. Learning to set limits, turning away from trying to change your partner, creating boundaries regardless of the results, and letting go of your dreams of a perfect relationship are not easy tasks. In fact, these things are so difficult that you should not employ the twelve Respect-Me Rules without a solid base of support. Chapters 9 and 10 will guide you in

"Codependency plays such a huge part in this sickness. I let this go on in my life for eighteen years, and I feel that my codependency was my crutch, if you will. Until I was able to stand UP for myself and face him and demand to be treated better, this was never going to go away. As long as I let him continue to blame me for his [abuse], he would."

—HADENOUGH,

FROM AN ABUSE FORUM

how to set your support structure in place. Do not think that reading this book is enough. It's not.

We have often repeated that your partner cannot verbally, mentally, or emotionally mistreat you if you respect your-self enough to prohibit *anyone* from mistreating you. Many people want so much to be a perfect person that they inadver-tently set themselves up for abuse. The truth is, many people do *not* allow themselves to be mis-treated, and they *aren't*. They respect themselves too much to become a target. Here is a great example that Shelly observed a few years ago that clearly shows how a woman can respect herself and not allow abuse.

At Busch Gardens, people can stroll through an aviary atrium while parrots fly down to perch on their shoulders or arms. It is a delightful display and a wonderful opportunity to interact with nature. Before entering, Shelly spotted a man standing stiffly at the exit, face red and fists clenched, with a look of disgust plastered on his face. There was a dollop of bird poo deposited on his shoulder. A woman stood before him, amused, and said, "No, I will not wipe the bird poo off your shoul-der. You can do it."

It was that simple. She did not do for him what he could do for himself, and she especially did not do it in response to his obvious anger. Her response was not angry, haughty, or taunting. It was matter-of-fact. What if she had responded codependently? That is to say, what if she had run to get a rag to clean off the bird poo and apologized for asking him to accompany her in the atrium in the first place? Then her partner would have learned the following:

1. If he gets angry, she will clean up his messes, whether or not she caused it.
2. He can blame her for choices he makes himself, such as going into the atrium.

It would have been a different scenario if he had said, "Honey, I can't reach this very well. Can you help me here?" In this case, helping her husband would be a very sweet thing, an act that partners want to do for each other. What differentiates this incident and places it in the abuse category is that he was fuming, angry, and demanding. His partner rightfully set and enforced her respect boundaries by saying no; she wasn't going to reward his bad behavior.

This woman and many like her are our heroes. Her response was simple and straightforward—not angry, not humiliating, not punishing, just simple and straightforward. Shelly thought a lot about that scene and wondered what this man would have done if he had been with his friends. Would he have gotten red in the face, clenched his fists, blamed them for taking him into the cage, and demanded that his buddies clean the bird poo off his shoulder? Probably not. More likely, he would laugh, make a joke, take a few lighthearted jabs from the guys, clean it off, and move on. Only abusers can turn a harmless, albeit embarrassing, incident into something their partners feel guilty for and responsible to clean up. And only codependents allow it!

Chapter Highlights

- There are three main ways we may develop codependent behaviors in our relationships: reliving trauma, adapting, and teaching the abuser that abuse works.
- Codependency cripples people and does not solve the abuse problem.
- Codependent behaviors are a very complicated topic. For the target, it means a loss of self in deference to the abuser, a delusional belief that doing things just right can earn the abuser's love and respect, and a mistaken conviction that she can somehow change him.
- In trying to stop the partner's abuse and control, a target ends up trying to control how the abuser feels about and treats her.
- Regardless of whether a target went into an abusive relationship as a codependent, once it turns abusive and she finds herself enmeshed in the abusive patterns, she becomes codependent.

Something to Think about

As emotionally satisfying as it is to understand how you got your-self into this fix and came to be codependent with your abusive partner, understanding the reasons doesn't do a single thing to stop it. The point now is to learn how to stop yourself from allowing anyone to mistreat you. The best approach to stop being a victim of abuse is to not allow it in the first place or, once you recognize that it has started, to immediately put a stop to it by setting boundaries and forbidding it to continue.

Notes

1. Charles L Whitfield, *Codependence—Healing the Human Condition* (Deerfield Beach: Health Communications, 1991), 6.
2. J. Humphrey and J. White, "Women's vulnerability to sexual assault from adolescence to young adulthood." *Journal of Adolescent Health* 27, no. 6 (1992): 419–24.
3. B.F. Skinner, *Contingencies of Reinforcement: A Theoretical Analysis* (Englewood Cliffs, NJ: Prentice-Hall, 1969).
4. Patricia Evans, *Controlling People: How to Recognize, Understand, and Deal with People Who Try to Control You* (Avon: Adams Media Corporation, 2002).

CHAPTER 7

The Benefits of Victimization

The most important thing is that you allow yourself the gift and the right to only be in environments that are respectful of you.

—PAMELA BREWER, MSW, PHD, LCSW-C

THE QUESTION MOST FREQUENTLY ASKED of someone in an abusive relationship is, "Why don't you leave?" The solution seems so simple, yet the reasons behind staying are exasperatingly complex. One reason is what is known as *secondary gain* in psychology. This refers to the positive reinforcement that occurs with "sick behaviors." For instance, hypochondriacs thrive off of the sympathy they get from others over their medical "problems." The class clown revels in the attention his antics elicit. And likewise, being a victim often results in copious sympathy, attention, concern, and help from others.

If a person wants to move from helpless victim to self-empowered target, then underlying motives such as these must be examined and understood. We reiterate that we are in no way trying to blame the target or say it is her fault the abuser chooses to abuse her. But we do recognize that psychology and the human psyche are complex, and the cause of behavior is multidetermined. Being overpowered by a physically powerful man is one thing, but taking verbal and emotional abuse stems directly from a lack of self-respect and personal responsibility. Many reasons we put up with an abuser and feel that we have to accept nasty behavior are below our conscious awareness. Nevertheless, that does not absolve us of the responsibility to change things once we understand what is going on. For these reasons we need to examine the underlying psychological dynamics of the abused.

Reasons for not leaving the relationship fall into two main categories—legitimate and dysfunctional. First we list some legitimate reasons that some people remain with their abusers even though the verbal and emotional abuse is extreme, humiliating, and traumatizing, making life a constant nightmare.

> "I work in the victim service office at the sheriff's office. Unfortunately, the story you had me read does not seem too far out of the norm. As I was reading the article, I continuously thought, 'Get out!' Why can't she see? Your program has brought to light a myriad of different reasonings behind why these targets stay in the abusive relationships."
>
> **—CRITICAL INCIDENT FIRST RESPONDER**

- *Economic dependency.* Not having a job, skills, work experience, money, shelter, transportation, or food is oftentimes scarier to the abused than staying with the abuser. For some women this can be time-sensitive. They may say, "I plan to leave him as soon as I finish my degree and get employment."
- *Impact on the children.* A woman may decide that she will suffer for the sake of the children. Although there is some evidence that it is better for the children if the mother leaves the abuser, ultimately it is her right to decide what is best.
- *Religious beliefs.* For instance, Catholics strongly believe that divorce is a sin, and many Catholics will avoid divorcing at all costs.
- *Fear.* There is a rare but nevertheless legitimate fear of being harmed when ending some relationships. Recall the case of O. J. and Nicole Simpson. Some women's intuition tells them that if they leave, their partners will harm them.

Of course, sometimes the above excuses are not legitimate reasons for staying in an abusive relationship—especially if it seems to be turning really ugly for the target. Often people put up with abuse because they feel powerless and trapped, believe that the good aspects of the relationship outweigh the disrespect, or simply have not been given the knowledge that they do not have to allow it.

Below are some dysfunctional reasons for staying in an abusive relationship. If you, as a target, can identify with any of these reasons (whether or not you consider them legitimate), you need to self-examine, learn better coping strategies, and take corrective action.

- *Relishing the victim role.* This would be someone who thrives on the copious attention and sympathy from others that being an abuse victim can elicit.

- *Traumatic bonding.* This is a psychological condition similar to the Stockholm Syndrome, whereby kidnapping victims come to identify with the cause of their captors. In traumatic bonding, the abused acquires a paradoxical bond with the abuser and, strangely, admires and protects him. It might be psychologically similar to what happens to cult members who worship their leader no matter how bizarre his beliefs and intense his abuse and exploitation of them becomes.

- *Fear of failure.* Women naturally take pride in their marriage, their husband's success, and their family. Divorce is stigmatized, and when a marriage dissolves, women often feel like they have failed. They fear that if they stop the abusive dance, there will be no relationship and they will be perceived by others as a failure or, worse, see themselves as a failure.

- *Self-pity.* This allows a woman to nurture herself at the expense of the abuser. It also contributes to the cycle of abuse when the abuser is in the apology phase of the cycle and is making up to the "victim." Its very passion is highly seductive to many targets.

- *Avoiding self-examination.* If he is the bad guy and you are the sweet and innocent victim, then you don't have to grow up. You must be taken care of and rescued. You must be saved by someone else. You don't have to take responsibility for managing your own life and examining your issues. It allows you to continue to blame the abuser and not see how you fit into the ongoing dysfunctional pattern.

> "WOW . . . I surely did not realize I had a pay-off in this situation; only to find out I have several."
>
> **—LEB**

- *Commiseration.* This has a social component. It makes the woman feel good and helps build allies, which allows her to avoid being criticized and even be seen as heroic. If a woman solves the problem, then she loses the benefits of being affiliated with the support group. The allies can be as formal as a community support group, as informal as family, or as loose as coworkers who commiserate about what they endure at home.

- *The need to be right.* The abuse reinforces that the target is right and the abuser is wrong. This seems logical because, in fact, he *is* wrong. She doesn't deserve the treatment he gives her. The problem with being right in this situation is that she continues to allow him to mistreat her so she can keep pointing out how wrong he is.

- *Reliving the trauma.* This occurs when someone unconsciously chooses an abusive partner, sometimes one after another. People have an unconscious psychological need to fix what went wrong in childhood. For instance, someone who had an alcoholic father may marry an alcoholic and firmly believe that with enough love and support, she can get her spouse to recover. Abuse might even feel more comfortable than being treated well because abuse was normal while growing up. Being treated right and not being abused, for some, falls outside of their comfort zone (see chapter 6).

- *He needs me.* The need to feel needed is very powerful. Who wouldn't feel sorry for someone whose partner abandoned him and left him lonely with no love or emotional support? Sometimes men will milk this motive with manipulative statements like, "I would kill myself if you left me" or "You're the only one who has ever loved me."

- *"But I love him."* This is often a sign of a distorted love map. A love map can be distorted in childhood and develop poorly. For example, a child who witnesses abuse between parents may come to see abuse as a sign of love.

- *Honeymoon payoff.* As callous as this may seem, the phase of abuse in which an abuser promises to never do it again, bears gifts, and begs forgiveness is very seductive to the target. This is when the partner says all the beautiful things a woman wants to hear and makes a concerted effort to make her dreams come true. He is intimate, tender, attentive, appreciative, and needy. Regardless of how many times the couple has danced this dance before, it remains attractive because the target wants to believe it so badly. The target minimizes the past and embraces the hope presented in this honeymoon part of the cycle. Giving up the abuse also means giving up the euphoria so prevalent in this phase.

It should be clear that all of these reasons are dysfunctional and need to be acknowledged and addressed. If you do not have the insight into whether any of these psychological dynamics, or others not covered here, are interfering with ending the abuse in a relationship, then professional counseling would likely help (see chapter 9). Don't let these dysfunctional psychological dynamics delay you from taking corrective action. The sooner you develop the skills to stop the abuse, the less likely the abuse will escalate past the point of no return.

Shelly can attest to the benefits of victimization from a personal standpoint.

> In my case, I allowed my husband to abuse me in the name of my spirituality. I was the morally superior one. The "better" person in the marriage. The more abusive he became, the harder I tried to "out-spirituality" him, to prove that I was righteous and he was spiritually bankrupt. I was earning reward points with God, and some-day all would come to see how saintly I was. Maybe, eventually, my husband would too, and we would become a wonderful and spiritual team together—but only after he apologized and acknowledged how wrong he had been.

We will end this chapter by listing many of the common excuses targets make for not leaving or stopping their abusers:

- *It will get better.* This is the eternal optimist who says, "He has so many other good qualities. I know he loves me, and he has promised he will get help and not do it anymore."
- *Other women would give anything to have what I have. I would be foolish to give up all of this.* For women in the hidden abusive relationships where the image of a successful career, family, and social life are all-important to the mate, it may appear to outsiders as if the abused partner "has it

made." If the man brings home a big paycheck, this adds to the illusion and makes it more difficult to pinpoint what is actually going on. Often the abused partner herself feels guilty for not appreciating all she has been given over a few "little" incidents.

- *Men can't control their impulses.* This denies the fact that abuse is a choice and everyone is responsible for their actions. The next relationship won't be any better and may be worse. This is our fatalist. Strangely, though, she is right. If a woman doesn't learn how to demand respect, the next relationship undoubtedly will mimic the current one.

- *Children need parents.* It is more accurate to say that children would like to have two parents but are most likely better off with one parent in a stable environment than with both in a dysfunctional, abusive one.

- *Drinking causes the abuse; it's not really him.* Drinking is also a choice. If it results in abuse, then it is the responsibility of the drinker to take action. If he is an alcoholic, he needs to get help through either a facility or a community support group such as AA. If he is not an alcoholic, then he needs to stop the behavior that causes him to act abominably out of love and respect and for the welfare of their family.

Essentially, the above are rationalizations and should not interfere with taking measures to take care of yourself, demanding the respect, care, and concern you deserve.

Chapter Highlights

- Sometimes people put up with abuse in their relationships because they are deriving secondary gain.
- Targets must perform a searching and fearless self-examination to discover their motives and determine if secondary gain or rationalizations are interfering with ending abuse and then take corrective action.

Something to Think about

How would you determine if your reason for putting up with abuse is legitimate? Is there ever really a legitimate reason for accepting abuse?

CHAPTER 8
Secrets: How and Why to Tell Them

Ultimately, truth-seeking is required, because shameful and discreditable information that remains hidden by deceptive secrecy will hurt the Secret Keepers and those who care about them until it becomes known, acknowledged, treated, and healed.

—JOHN HOWARD PRIN

TEACHING THE PARTNER that abuse works or trying to change *him* are not the only ways in which a target contributes to the abuse pattern. Enabling is another behavior that we hear about in addictions and, in contrast to control, it manifests itself because few want to admit what is really going on in a dysfunctional relationship. Enabling is when the target covers up, makes excuses for, and keeps silent about all the abusive behaviors she lives with. It means that the target conceals the abusive behaviors, thus protecting her abuser from the consequences that would naturally occur if all were out in the open.

Secret-keeping is the form of enabling that targets fall prey to without realizing how unhealthy it is for the whole family. This type of enabling is born of rationalization. It is easier for the target to deny that she is truly being abused than to give up her dreams. The abuser may brainwash his partner into thinking that "telling" is a betrayal of the relationship. In addition, there is the component of *benefits* that we spoke of in chapter 7. If we expose the relationship secrets, the payoff from the interactions may go away.

Enabling is often insidious and begins slowly. A partner may say, "What goes on in this family stays in this family." A target is fed the line that she is betraying her husband and family by publicly displaying their "dirty laundry." Sometimes the line is more blatant: "If you tell your mother I locked you in the closet, you will not see her this Christmas." Or he may use the kids as a threat: "I'll take the kids away from you if you make up lies about me." (They are not lies, but in abuse, the abuser most often sees them that way and says that you are crazy, you imagined it, you are telling lies, or you exaggerate to gain sympathy.)

It's not your job to keep your abuser's secrets. But often you don't even know that the secrets you are keeping are really secrets at all. What are the types of secrets that can keep the relationship sick?

Verbal Abuse Secrets

He yells at you continually, calls you horrible names, or constantly speaks to you sarcastically or in demeaning terms.

Emotional Abuse Secrets

He threatens you or your children, hurts or threatens to hurt your pet, threatens to kill you or himself, withholds money, isolates you from family and friends, or monitors and controls your actions.

Sexual Secrets

He is addicted to pornography, masturbation, or sexual intercourse (cyber or physical), forsakes intimacy with you for other sexual pleasures, or makes you engage in humiliating sexual acts.

What would be the advantage, you may ask, of telling the relationship secrets? After all, the categories above do seem like the type of things you don't want your family or neighbors to know. For one thing, once the people around you know that you are living with abuse, it will be harder for you to return to your old patterns after you explain to your partner that you respect yourself and will not allow the shabby treatment any longer. Shedding light on abuse is one of the surest ways to remove the bull's-eye from your back. Remember Respect-Me Rule #9: Record Everything. When Shelly's husband thought she was recording their arguments, his behavior was vastly more controlled than when he thought no one would ever know about it. In addition, when you tell others what you are going through, you may receive important feedback that otherwise would not have been available.

One woman we know, Jeanette, was in an abusive relationship, and few suspected anything. Jeanette knew something was wrong but wasn't quite sure what was going on. Her mother came to visit, and Jeanette mentioned in an off-handed way how she wasn't allowed to take a bath while her husband was at home. "Allowed?" her mother asked. Jeanette's mother did a little probing and found out that Jeanette was suffering from all sorts of abusive treatment. Her husband did things like impose time limits on how long she could be at the grocery store, forbid her to answer the door when he was not home, accuse her of affairs with others, including a female cousin and the postman, desert her in strange places without transportation when he was angry, and sell her car to buy his own. Fortunately, Jeanette had a wise mom who immediately began talking to her about abuse, self-respect, and ways to take care of herself. Because of this, when her husband turned from emotional abuse to physical violence, Jeanette had enough insight to put a plan in place and had no trouble leaving the relationship without guilt.

> "Here's where NOT keeping secrets is a BIG, HUGE step in healing. Embracing reality will help heal you. It may mean facing fear, but there is no reason you should continue to be MENTALLY tortured by the verbal and emotional 'sleeper bombs' abusers plant in your mind and soul. Tell, tell tell."
>
> **—BARBARA S.**

We Are Only as Safe as the Secrets We Don't Keep

"We are only as sick as our secrets," they say. What they don't say is, "We are only as safe as the secrets we don't keep." Serial killer Gary Ridgway wanted to kill his second wife, Marcia, but didn't for only one reason. During an argument, Gary had violently grabbed and choked her from behind. She was not a codependent, nor was she caught in the cycle of abuse, so she did not keep his secret! Marcia told her parents and friends that her husband had tried to kill her. At one time, she filed a restraining order.[1] They divorced, but Marcia lived to tell her tale. Why? Years later, when he was caught, Ridgway told detectives that he indeed wanted to kill Marcia. There was only one reason he did not stage her death as he had done with other women: because she told so many people, he deduced they would suspect him and he might get caught. Telling the "secret" saved Marcia's life.[2]

When you decide to tell, you may invite criticism from many, including your partner's family and possibly yours, depending on their concept of marriage. They

> "It wasn't any fun being married to an abuser and sex addict, but it was less fun fighting for my emotional health, only to face our culture's obsession with protecting the guilty. One of the biggest issues I faced after discovering my husband's exhibitionism and joining COSA, the group for the spouses of sex addicts, was that I will surely be blamed for telling his secret."
>
> **—SHELLY M.**

may come down on you as if *you* are in the wrong and say, "How could you make life difficult for him? Embarrass him? Humiliate him? Risk his job? His reputation?" They make you believe you should protect the abuser and that if you were a good wife, then he wouldn't abuse you.

Exposing your ex or your current partner is necessary so that you both can change. If the abuse problem is kept in the dark, your partner will be protected from the most powerful of consequences, and you enable the problem rather than enforce your boundaries. Talk yourself out of feeling guilty about telling. Consider it carefully, get a base in recovery, and then figure out who to tell and the best way to do it.

Your Silence Is His Tool

Silence is a powerful tool that your abuser uses to maintain his stranglehold on the relationship and to keep you from seeing how insane it all is. Without your silence, he cannot continue to control you with abuse. How long do you think a father would tolerate his son-in-law telling his daughter at Thanksgiving dinner, "You spilled the gravy on your shirt again, you clumsy ox. Were you raised in a barn?" If an abuser abuses in public, it usually won't last long.

Most forms of abuse occur behind closed doors. In public, the abuser curbs his own behavior for fear of exposure. Additionally, when abuse is in the open, the target gets feedback from witnesses that helps her evaluate the situation more accurately. A target may have adapted over time so she doesn't readily recognize disrespectful treatment, but her family and friends will recognize it if told what is going on. In the example of Jeanette, she knew something wasn't right and was able to tell her mother a few things, including how she wasn't allowed to take a bath if her husband wasn't home. Her mother helped her figure out the rest. If Jeanette had hidden her misgivings, then when her husband began hitting, she may have bought into the notion that she was the cause. In many cases, when a target brings mistreatment out in the open, others can explain how crazy it is to allow such behavior to continue. Exposing abuse is usually the starting point to get the support that is needed to rebuild self-respect.

Children are another reason that domestic cruelty should not be kept hidden. Children pay the highest price and often grow up to continue the pattern. (Remember that one form of ending up in this type of relationship comes from reliving the trauma, as discussed in chapter 6.) Not only can you create abusers by raising kids in such an environment, but you can also create targets. Witnessing abuse at a young age can lead to involvement in dysfunctional relationships later in life, and a target who keeps such secrets increases the likelihood that this unfortunate outcome will occur.

Do Not Confuse Privacy with Secret Keeping

John Prin explains that keeping things private is not bad or immoral. Only keeping secrets that are deceitful or intentionally concealing what is shameful—such as treating your partner with disdain and humiliation—are unhealthy. Prin says:

> Privacy can be defined as *limiting unwanted access by others.* Privacy means, something kept from the view of strangers. People rightly seek protection for the innocent, harmless, legitimate activities of life. One keeps a file of taxes private, or underwear in a drawer or prescriptions in a medicine cabinet. We take for granted the legitimacy of hiding silver from burglars and personal documents from snoopers and busybodies, all meant for nobody else's eyes.
>
> - Privacy is an act of choosing healthy boundaries and staying comfortably within them.
> - Secret-keeping is an act of hiding from the embarrassment of disclosing things shameful or discreditable.[3]

Unhealthy secrecy shields shameful and deceitful behavior—things that go beyond the bounds of decency. Keeping a secret about a surprise birthday party or a personal conversation is one thing. Keeping secrets that destroy your self-worth is another. An example of destructive secret-keeping would be if your spouse smashed chocolate cake in your face while screaming, "Glutton, I wish I'd never married a pig like you," and then telling you that if you tell, you are betraying him.

How Does One Go About Telling?

You may struggle at each juncture when telling becomes an option. You might want to begin with a support group or counselor. Use a safe environment to begin telling your story. You may want to start with your mother or best friend. Initially, you might choose to reveal things on an as-needed basis. You may wonder, "Will I hate myself if he is humiliated because I told? Am I making too much out of it, and will this make us look bad in front of others? Am I betraying the relationship? Am I admitting failure? Shouldn't I handle this on my own?"

Take telling the secrets slowly so that you don't make mistakes you will regret later. Breaking the silence is necessary, yet it is also a delicate matter, and you may want to have a good foundation in recovery before you shout out to the world that your partner is an abuser and that you are a target. You definitely want to avoid using telling as a way

---

"Eventually the aggressiveness and sexual deviance would come back, time and again, only to be followed by pathetic, tearful apologies and promises that it would never happen again. It always did, so I left. Before leaving, I visited every neighbor of mine because I was scared of the consequences. I sought legal advice as well (who pointed me in the direction of telling neighbors because of the sexual stuff). After I left, one of the neighbors visited him and told him what I had said. He was very angry, of course, that I had let out his secret (just read your secret bit). I'm glad I told, because he will in no way now continue to perve on all the teens in his street and terrify his neighbors. It was the right thing to do."

—SANDRA P.

---

to garner allies who will see you as a victim and label him as bad. The point of telling is to end the abuse and practice the Respect-Me Rules. It is so *you* don't enable the abuse, not to make others hate him. This may be the person you will spend the rest of your life with, and you don't need to polarize everyone. For that reason, sometimes it is best not to tell those closest to you, such as family, because they may be unable to forgive your partner. You must decide what is best based on your situation.

Ways to Tell

Join a support group. Most support groups are free, and you can learn a lot about what is going on and about other resources. This is usually a safe place to begin telling your story. If you are in a small town where everyone knows everyone and feel unsure about joining a program, you might consider joining an online group.

Participate in your support group's public demonstrations, especially if it's in the same town where you live. Shelly marched in a Take Back the Night parade for her support group and gave a speech explaining how emotional abuse is as bad or worse than physical violence. Many women shook her hand afterward because they identified with what she said and she gave them hope.

Tell the truth to people who ask. Don't sugarcoat in order to protect his job or reputation. You don't need to run around volunteering info about your verbally abusive partner, but when appropriate, give facts. When is it appropriate? Read the following examples:

- You go to lunch with the girls. They ask why you were late and you answer truthfully, "Oh, my husband hid my keys and it took me twenty minutes to find them." You continue the conversation for as long as they are interested.
- You take your necklace to the jeweler because the clasp is broken. When the jeweler, who has known your family for years, asks what happened, you explain that your husband ripped it off in a fit of rage.
- Your in-laws call and ask why you didn't come over with their son for dinner last Sunday. You explain matter-of-factly that he has been raging at you and that when he rages, he erratically drives eighty miles an hour and that you won't get into a vehicle with him when he acts like that. In addition, if he gets a ticket,

he will blame it on you and get even madder. You no longer choose to subject yourself to that kind of behavior from him.

All of these scenarios are honest explanations to honest questions and are appropriate ways to break the silence.

List abusive behavior in a divorce. If you end up in divorce, don't go for a no-fault if your state allows you to list the reasons. Shelly was able to file for divorce with cause. Although she eventually settled for a no-fault for financial reasons, her story is still a matter of court record and can be cited as such. If her ex's new partner ever sees the divorce papers, she will know exactly what he is capable of doing.

Be honest with your kids. Explain as much as you can, based on their ages and circumstances. Don't lie to them. They already know things aren't right. Lying only confuses them.

Tell your counselor. If your counselor insists that you are half the problem because you won't compromise, get a counselor who under-stands verbal/emotional abuse. You are part of the problem, but your actions do not cause him to treat you badly. What you allow to happen to you perpetuates his nasty and belittling behavior. Abuse is not some-thing that you must learn to compromise on. Abuse must stop—period. You cannot meet him halfway. If your counselor doesn't get it, find another counselor to tell your story to.

Tell your mother, father, siblings, and friends everything. Although you must judge each situation for appropriateness, when you don't tell those that can be your resources, you give your abuser power and become his enabler. The next time you think you are "protecting" your mate or marriage by not telling about the maltreatment, remember that you will suffer, your children will suffer, and you will teach the abuser that treating you badly is acceptable behavior.

Keep a detailed diary. This will help remind you when you forget how bad it is and can help you see the abuse patterns. You can also use it later if you need evidence in court. Dated journals are court admissible. Shelly's journal was a godsend. When her husband tried to "forget" what he had done, she could read to him the date and time that he had done it. Her journal kept her from believing him when he said, "You're crazy. It never happened. You blow things out of proportion."

Publish. Write an article. Create your own website with your story and pictures. Post all pictures that relate—things he tore up, the car he crashed, all his boy-toys that he purchased while you went without, or whatever illustrates your life together. If you don't feel confident in your writing skills, blog about it. Blogs are for the lay person, and you don't have to be a talented writer. You can make it private, if you wish, so that only those who you allow can see it. Write a song, a poem, or whatever will illustrate his rage. Then post it somewhere. Write press releases for your support group and use your marriage or partnership as a concrete example. Publishing like this also helps other women know they are not alone.

Call the police. If he punches a hole in the wall, destroys property, hurts your pet, or threatens to kill you or himself, call the police and file a report. In some states, like Colorado, a person can be arrested for destroying his own property or acting in a threatening manner in a domestic situation. In some states, like Virginia, people can do anything they want to their own property, so you must check your state laws.

Telling can be tricky. You have to tell in order to not enable. You need to tell so that you can get support. If you keep his secrets, you keep the relationship sick. Yet the point is not to build an army against the abuser. It is not to gain pleasure from tattling, as we did when we were kids. The guidelines are as follows:

- Tell the truth without embellishment.
- Tell when it is appropriate.
- Check your motives. Don't tell in order to punish.
- Is there a good reason for telling, or do you only want to shock someone?
- Do you need guidance, or are you taking pleasure in making him look bad?
- Are you sharing with a friend so she can remind you not to allow disrespect, or do you want an ally in a power struggle against your abuser?

Only you can answer these questions because only you know what's in your heart. But remember, silence is the enemy—silence between you and those who might be resources and bring support to you and your family.

Here are ten great reasons to break the silence:

1. It's not your job to keep his secrets.
2. You're only as sick as your secrets.

3. Secrets are dangerous.
4. You take away one of the abuser's greatest tools when you break the silence.
5. You can discuss things openly with your children with the hope of preventing them from growing up to relive the trauma.
6. The more people you tell, the harder it will be for you to go back to the way it was.
7. Vindication. People will now realize you have good reason to act the way you do.
8. If you end up leaving, you might prevent him from abusing someone else.
9. Be a role model. Other women (or men) may stop playing victim when they know what you went through.
10. Your partner will have a harder time sustaining the abuse if everyone knows.

Chapter Highlights

- When you keep his secrets, you enable him to continue to abuse you.
- Telling others about the abuse helps you to end it by enlisting valuable social resources to empower yourself.

Something to Think about

When you cover up for and protect your partner's disrespect and maltreatment of you, you in essence live a double life. Your greatest resources may not even suspect that you need help. By enabling your partner, you blur your judgment and support his faulty reality. This faulty reality is not only toxic to you, your partner, and your relationship, but it is also toxic to your children. What secrets are you keeping, and who is it appropriate to tell that can help empower you?

Notes

1. Mark Prothero with Carlton Smith, *Defending Gary: Unraveling the Mind of the Green River Killer* (San Francisco: Jossey-Bass, 2006), 274, 340, 370.
2. Robert Keppel, *The Riverman: Ted Bundy and I Hunt for the Green River Killer* (New York: Pocket Books, 1995–2005), 521–22, 445.

3. John Howard Prin, "Are Secrets Good or Bad?" *John Prin Articles*, accessed February 10, 2010, http://www.johnprin.com/articles/art-secretsgoodorbad.htm. Appeared in *The Phoenix*, (St. Paul, February 2004).

CHAPTER 9

Choosing the Right Therapist

Things do not change. We change.

—HENRY DAVID THOREAU

AFTER SUFFERING THROUGH the terrible ordeal of an abusive relationship, most people will seek counseling to help them heal and work through any residual issues. For some, there are deeper issues that need to be resolved. These people need to gain insight into why they picked an unhealthy person to be in a relationship with in the first place. Well-adjusted people spot abusers with ease and pass right by them (see chapter 12). But then there are those who are attracted to an abuser for reasons sometimes unknown to themselves. Mental health professionals are aware of the reasons people behave in this self-defeating manner and can provide assistance in gaining the psychological knowledge, insight, and skills to fix it before their clients blindly make the same mistake in future relationships.

There are also those who are naïve and think, "But I just made an innocently poor relationship choice and don't need psychotherapy. It's not going to happen again." Not likely! Social psychologists call this the overconfidence effect. They find that most people rate themselves as better than others on all personal attributes and abilities, especially in their ability to judge others' character. Most abuse targets need psychotherapy even if they think they don't. At any rate, counseling is not likely to hurt anyone and usually helps. Both Shelly (the lay self-help type) and Dr. Marshall (the professional) have trouble understanding why someone who is involved in an abusive relationship would think she does not need therapy. Those who are emotionally healthy and coping

101

well in life usually do not pick abusive partners. Yes, some people can be fooled, and there is the fact that many partners train an otherwise nice person that being mean gets them what they want, but our subconscious radar almost always seeks out and finds someone who is a perfect match for our unresolved

> "Nearly three months ago, my wife moved out and is now living with her parents in an attempt to see if our marriage can be salvaged. I have since been seeking every different thing that I can find to help me to learn to handle my anger, including counseling, online support boards, and just a couple weeks ago I found an Anger Alternatives group that I hope will help."
>
> **—RICH H.**

issues and underlying neuroses. Generally, if someone is psychologically healthy enough that she does not need psychotherapy, then she could have found a nurturing, nonabusive partner. Likewise, she would understand that being nice to him when he is mean will not create a happy union.

Some people do not need or want psychotherapy. Some even refuse it. We're not going to be the ones who tell you a self-help book is sufficient for you and that you do not need therapy. It would be professionally irresponsible. Life is too complex, people are too emotionally caught up in their relationship problems to always think clearly, and people have too many blind spots about themselves. This book helps you *begin* to understand the dynamics of abusive relationships and offers some skills in helping you stop the blatant abuse. However, if you want to completely unravel the complexity of your relationship dynamics, understand your underlying psychological structure, and identify the role your issues play in your patterns, then you need to see a therapist. If you choose not to, that's your right. If you are aware of the red flags covered in chapter 12, then you may be able to avoid repeating history.

Finally, there are those who are so emotionally downtrodden and psychologically battered that they can't wait to get into therapy. Their self-esteem is shot. They are depressed and anxious. They can't sleep. Life is seen as drudgery and not worth living. So what should they do to find a good therapist, and what do they look for during therapy to make sure it's working? Since rapport is the basis of most effective therapy, choosing the right therapist is essential. This means finding a therapist who is skilled, makes you feel comfortable, and is effective. In this chapter we will present some psychotherapy basics to help you achieve your therapeutic goals.

Define Your Issues

What are the problems? Verbal abuse is likely to be a major one. Is your partner going to attend sessions with you, or have you decided to go alone? If he is going, what are other problems that need to be worked on besides verbal and emotional abuse—parenting styles, sexual issues, substance abuse, infidelity, communication, or fighting over finances? Are you trying to save the relationship, or are you seeking divorce counseling? If you come to the first session having thought about some of these issues, then you will not waste any time and should make faster progress.

Therapists' Credentials

There seems to be a dizzying array of different types of therapists out there, with an endless list of different initials after their names. There are counselors, psychologists, clinical social workers, psychiatrists, pastoral counselors, and marriage and family counselors. Fortunately, the complexity can be reduced to four basic questions:

1. Is the therapist licensed?
2. Does he have expertise and experience with abuse issues?
3. Does he accept my insurance?
4. Is he recommended by others?

You can find the answers to these questions with some quick research. Start with the Internet. Go to your insurance company's website. Click the choices that guide you to a list of mental health care providers in your area. There should be a long list. All of them are properly credentialed and are likely good therapists. Oftentimes, there's even a list of their respective areas of expertise. Just to be sure, you should ask for recommendations. Most people are eager to tell others what they know of the reputations of professionals, whether they be doctors, lawyers, plastic surgeons, judges, or therapists.

Does it make a difference what his discipline is, whether he is a counselor, clinical social worker, or psychologist? Not really. Research

"Psychotherapy hasn't really worked at times. I still go to a counselor to learn about what my issues were and how to talk about things. I'm also doing research on what abuse is. Had a sketchy idea since I automatically blamed myself for everything that went wrong in relationships and would try to make it better or change the other person. Along with counseling, this is working."

—ANDREA

indicates that experience is more important. There are excellent and weak therapists in all the respective professions. A degree and license is necessary, but not sufficient, to be a good therapist.

Be careful to avoid unlicensed therapists. They are everywhere. One survey found there were six thousand in Colorado alone.[1] They can be dangerous and do not have to conform to any code of ethical conduct. They use titles like therapist, hypnotherapist, or life coach because they are not protected terms so the use of those titles is not illegal. Professional associations such as the American Psychological Association, the American Psychiatric Association, the American Counseling Association, and the National Association of Social Workers have lobbied state legislatures to pass laws making their titles protected terms. Therefore, anyone using a protected title such as psychologist, psychiatrist, clinical social worker, or licensed professional counselor who has not gone through the rigorous training, testing, and licensing requirements is breaking the law. It is not necessary to do extensive background checks on your prospective therapist if you get his name from a list of your insurance company's providers. Your insurance company has done that job for you by recredentialing their providers every few years.

Whether you seek counseling for only yourself or for yourself and your partner, it is crucial that you find a counselor who is trained in verbal and emotional abuse. Many counselors specialize in abusive relationships and are trained to recognize abusive patterns as couples sit in therapy. Many are not and will only recognize abuse if they see a black eye or read a hospital report about a broken arm. If you don't find a professional with a deep understanding of verbal and emotional abuse, chances are you will be abused even as you are seeking help in the therapeutic relationship.

A properly trained counselor can read between the lines and identify maltreatment as it unfolds. At that point, he will generally arrange
to see the two people separately as well as together. The purpose for this
is two-fold:

- It allows the abused to state things in a nonjudgmental or
  nonpunishing setting and provides her with a safe place to gain
  skills and explore options.
- It gives the counselor the ability to explore the partner's abusive
  behavior in a setting where he won't be embarrassed in front of
  the target, lowering the likelihood that he will drop out or go
  home and take it out on her.

Additionally, a good therapist will not allow the therapy itself to be
abusive by permitting the abuser to carry on in sessions (for example,
lie, minimize his abuse, or give her looks as if to say "don't bring that
up") or worse, permitting himself to minimize what is occurring. Ask a
prospective professional the following questions:

- Have you read more than one book on verbal and emotional
  abuse?
- Do you keep up with the research on verbal abuse and not just
  physical violence?
- Have you been certified, or do you have continuing education
  credits for verbal and emotional abuse counseling methods?
- Have you run anger management courses?
- Have you attended workshops on verbal abuse?

You have probably been told that a therapist does not take sides, but
he must for verbal abuse. Do not let your counselor say, "It takes two"
and proclaim that compromise is the answer. It is not. The therapist
must take sides, not between partners, but against *any abusive behavior*.
He must clearly and concisely let both parties know that abuse is never
warranted and should not be tolerated. If, after beginning therapy, you
notice any of the following problems with the therapist, you will want
to seriously consider dropping him and looking for another, better
trained professional.

1. Does the therapist allow the abuser to see himself as a victim so
    that you begin to take the heat for his unacceptable behavior?
    For example, does he allow your partner to say, "If she had

waited to tell me until I had relaxed . . . if she had said it differently . . . if she had just got home on time," thus making the target the one who triggered the abuse?

2. Is the therapist able to see that the root of the problem is abuse and not any other underlying causes? If your therapist thinks that solving childhood issues will stop abuse today, you want a different therapist. Once he identifies the problem as abuse itself and provides both of you skills for stopping it, you can delve into the past and identify lifelong patterns. Learning why your partner does it and why you allow it are great approaches after the pain, hurt, and degradation stop. Understanding your past does not stop the abuse today.

3. Does the therapist encourage you to trust your partner before it is earned, as if trusting your abuser will make him trustworthy?

4. Does the therapist believe you? Or does he say, "We all have different perspectives. If you could see it from his side, it might give you both greater understanding of each other"? Some things you don't have to understand from your partner's perspective. These include (but are not limited to) being called demeaning names, being accused of having an affair, or being accused of betraying your partner when you talk to your mother. These actions are plain and simple abuse, and you must not allow it to happen. Nor should a therapist suggest that you need to understand your abuser's perspective.

Last, keep in mind that if you do not click with the therapist you have chosen, try another. Don't let the therapy itself add to the already existing abuse or cause more trauma and erosion of self-respect just because it is coming from a professional. Don't worry about hurting the therapist's feelings. It happens regularly and therapists are used to it. You may not click because you see that the professional doesn't understand abuse, or it might be something as simple as chemistry. Dr. Marshall can't stand the strain of trying to make progress with a client who is just not a good match for his style. If the client does not take the initiative to find someone else, then Dr. Marshall will politely say, "You know, I realize that I am just not skilled enough to help you make good progress with this problem, but I can refer you to someone who has more experience in this area."

Fees

If your insurance covers counseling, expect to make about a $20 co-pay for each session. If you pay out of pocket, the cost may range from about $50 to $150 per session. If you are uninsured and full pay is too much for you financially, ask the therapist if he has a sliding scale. Most do. Expect to pay around $10 to $50 on the sliding scale. If you do not have sufficient financial resources, ask the therapist if he does pro bono (free) work. If the answer is no, don't forget about seeking free counseling at your community mental health agency. Most will not turn you away.

Keep a few things in mind about insurance companies. In order to get them to cover counseling services, they require that counseling be "medically necessary," and they require "prior authorization." If you tell your insurance company that you are seeking marriage counseling, they will deny the prior authorization because they will not deem it medically necessary. To them, medical necessity means a mental illness. This sounds like a dire term, but it also includes emotional conditions such as depression and anxiety. Odds are, you are suffering from depression or anxiety if you have been subjected to verbal and emotional abuse. If you are, your therapist will submit the bill to the insurance company with a diagnosis of Adjustment Disorder with anxiety, depression, or both, and the insurance company will gladly cover the services.

Other Considerations

Do you prefer a male or female counselor? Generally, women are more comfortable with a female counselor. This is understandable, particularly if a female target's abuser is male. It is important to keep in mind that marriage and family counselors have specific training in family systems and relationships, if that is your main issue. If your main concern is working on yourself rather than the relationship and dealing with such issues as self-esteem, trauma, codependency, anger management, addiction, anxiety, or depression, then other types of therapists would be suitable.

Once you have found a therapist, ask yourself if the counselor does the following things:

- Acts professionally
- Is sensitive to your needs

"I didn't look for a great therapist but a male therapist because I felt my husband would be more comfortable—again, I was taking care of him and not me. Turned out the therapist had as many issues as my husband, and they both yelled at me for being unreasonable. That was two weeks before my husband was found in bed with a seventeen-year-old. The therapist never saw it coming."

—JEANETTE

- Promptly returns your phone calls
- Does not talk about his own problems during a session
- Does not try to establish a personal relationship with you outside of therapy
- Does not cross intimacy boundaries
- Makes you a priority during sessions (such as not answering the phone when you are present)

If you can answer yes to all of these questions, then you likely have a good therapist. If not, immediately find a different, more professional therapist.

Some people will advise you to inquire about the therapist's training, degrees, and theoretical approach, but though it is imperative that you ask questions about his verbal and emotional abuse background, asking about degrees and how he approaches therapy may be awkward and less fruitful than gathering recommendations and information from others about the therapist's reputation. If the therapist is listed on the insurer's provider list, then he is almost certainly well trained, licensed, and in good professional standing. As in any other profession, some people are very good at what they do. Others are not as good because of such things as motivation, personal problems, or plain old personality clashes with you or your partner. All therapists learn the behavioral science of therapy in school. Some just apply it better than others. Their reputations will emerge along with experience in the field, and that reputation is going to be the most valuable of any type of information you need to know about them.

Chapter Highlights

- Most people who are in abusive relationships would benefit from professional psychotherapy or counseling to speed up the acquisition of abuse-stopping skills, help mend emotional scars, and fix related relationship problems.
- Finding the right therapist is paramount. The therapist should have specific skills relevant to abusive relationships. You should feel comfortable with the therapist, and he should behave professionally.

Something to Think about

If you think you don't need psychotherapy, are you making a realistic appraisal of your intelligence and insight, or are you rationalizing and setting yourself up to fall into another abusive relationship?

Note

1. Steve Andreas, "How NLP Was Saved From Regulation." *Institute for the Advanced Studies of Health*, accessed March 18, 2010, http://www.nlpiash.org/Articles/RecentArticles/tabid/250/EntryID/15/Default.aspx.

CHAPTER 10

Support Groups

Domestic abuse goes in one direction; it gets worse.
You don't have to wait until you are hit to say "no" to
domestic abuse.

—DR. JEANNE KING, PhD

EMOTIONAL ABUSE AFFECTS ALL INVOLVED. This includes your loved ones, friends, children, pets, partner, and most especially yourself. All types of abuse are toxic. When directed at you, abuse can be confusing, make you feel crazy, and keep you off balance. In healing from its impact, you need support, support, support. The authors encourage you to reach out to obtain this support and advice while learning how to break the cycle. If you *don't* reach out for support and learn how to break the cycle—your cycle—the abuse will get worse and you will feel worse about yourself.

More than likely, if you are being abused, you have been isolated from your family, friends, and social networks, with the exception of the ones your partner allows. You will need to end your isolation, even if he has threatened your family and friends and even if he has threatened to leave you or to take the children or other such threats. (If he threatens physical violence, take it seriously and immediately seek professional help from a domestic violence professional.) You need to gain strength and clarity and begin the process of respecting yourself and your decisions. It is much easier to do all this with an extensive support network than to attempt it all alone.

In the last chapter we asked you to seek professional help. That is important and will help a lot, provided you have located the right therapist. However, even if you haven't yet found professional help, you can still begin the process of stopping abuse as long as you have the right support. This means a community or a self-help support group of some kind. You have two main arenas to explore:

- **Virtual:** A computer chat room, forum, email support group, instant messaging, or online workshop.
- **Face-to-face:** An agency-run community support group, twelve-step support group, or faith-based religious help.

Support groups are not all equal. Some will focus more on blaming the perpetrator, such as domestic violence groups that tell you to secret things away and how to avoid provoking the abuser. Domestic violence groups *should* focus on physical safety and how to prevent outbursts. But with verbal and emotional abuse, we focus on change within the relationship, not refuge from the relationship. Some religious groups reinforce a man's "right" to rule the family, and some programs focus on family background as being the problem, which makes you feel better about how you got there but does little in the way of providing solutions. Other groups, the ones we encourage you to find, will focus on you not allowing anyone to treat you badly.

It is the responsibility of the target to decide whether a group is appropriate for what she wants to accomplish. Remember chapter 5, where we discussed the target's abuse cycle? If you are still stuck in the anger, blame, or depression stages of the abuse cycle, then you will identify with the groups that call you a victim or a survivor. If you are ready for change, then you will want to avoid the groups that blame your upbringing or partner, or delve into pity and heap on gobs of sympathy. We all know abuse is wrong. We all know abuse hurts. But it doesn't go away because someone feels sorry for you, you are good enough, or you understand that your parents didn't raise you right or that his parents didn't raise him right. Abuse goes away when you respect yourself enough to put a stop to it.

Since part of your job now is to gain strength and learn to take care of yourself, the authors are not going to tell you where to go for your support. They will guide you to do this job yourself. They will steer you in the right direction, and you will do the work, make the ultimate decisions, and learn to practice the principles you are learning. This is the beginning of your new way of life, where *you are in charge* and you make the decisions.

Safety First

First, go online. If you don't have a computer at home or don't feel that you can use it privately, find one you can use safely. This may be at your mother's or friend's house, your work (make sure that you have permission to use it for personal things during breaks and after hours), a community center, the library, or a domestic violence shelter or agency. Seeking help online is one of the most useful ways to find and gain support. However, computers and email can be another way for an abusive partner to monitor, control, accuse, and abuse you. You may decide that everything you do is out in the open, so you don't care if your partner sees what you are doing online. You may want to use this as a prompt (Respect-Me Rule #11) to show him or her that life is changing. Or you may decide his need to control what you do on the Internet is another form of abuse that you will not tolerate. You can go either way on this. It is your decision.

> "I have been married to a verbal abuser for thirteen years. Tonight I got sucked in again, but instead of crying and ruining my evening, I went to the Internet. I have, of course, tried to school myself on verbal abuse in the past, and that's what drove me to the Internet. I said to myself, 'Look for some help. Don't let this ruin your days off. You know it's not you.' I am excited about your work and thank you for cheering me up! I feel better already. It's not me, and I am not alone!"
>
> **—REBECCA**

If you are afraid of your partner and think that some things might push him to violence, use only a safe computer. This, of course, will be one outside of your home. Don't use your home computer unless you are very good with computers and know how to cover your tracks. If you choose to use your home computer, gain some Internet security knowledge first. Womenslaw.org and many other domestic abuse sites give detailed instructions on how to clear your computer's Internet browser and email account from showing evidence of you seeking help.

Open an email account for yourself at Google, Yahoo, or any web-based email program. Make sure it is *web-based* (email is stored on their server and not the computer you are using). There are a number of free web-based email services you can use. Do not use any of your real identifying information if you want to remain private or if you decide that you will not offer your partner the chance to abuse you through snooping in your private place. Here is a list of a few free web-based email programs:

- **Gmail:** http://www.gmail.com
- **Hotmail:** http://www.hotmail.com
- **Yahoo!Mail:** http://mail.yahoo.com
- **Mail.com:** http://www.mail.com
- **Hushmail:** http://www.hushmail.com
- **Mail City:** http://mail.lycos.com
- **Fastmail:** http://www.fastmail.fm

Some of these may force you to list another email in order to open an account. If you can't use a friend's email to open your new account, Hushmail allows you to open an email account without giving another email address. Your partner may still be able to read your email if you do not log out or if you choose a password that he can guess. The safest way to use a new email address is from a computer that the abuser does not have access to. Go to www.womenslaw.org and click on the "Internet Security" section or go to any site that tells you how to maintain your privacy while online.

This is your private and personal email. This is your healing place and your recovery base. Make it safe and secure. In setting up your email, use an identifying name to remind you what your goal is. It should reflect the principle of Respect-Me Rule #1: "Respect Me. I Deserve and Demand Respect." Here are some examples of the types of phrases you might use to express your newfound inner goals:

- RespectMe
- IntoMyOwn
- TargetNoMore
- RespectKathy

Once you have your new email account, scour the Internet for support. Find a search engine (Google, Yahoo, Start Page) and type in something like

- domestic abuse support group
- emotional abuse support

- online support for domestic abuse
- Internet verbal abuse support

Once again, steer away from groups that use the words *victim, survivor, adult child,* and *inner child* anywhere in their description. If they are using those words in the title or description of the group, they are more likely to attract those in the "be angry, blame, and get away" mental state rather than the "teach others how to treat me" mental state. This is not a hard-and-fast rule, but the names do reflect the type of help you will receive. For our purposes, we want to concentrate on groups that show you how to change your patterns. For instance, review the names of these three forums we found on the Internet:

Victims of Abuse Stand Up
"We the victims can take a stand & finally speak out & share our stories."[1]

Weasel-free
"Weasel Free in 2003!! Or Weasel no more in 2004, I will survive in 2005 or for those of us who haven't become "unstuck" yet "I found the fix and left in 2006."[2]

Women's Emotional Abuse Support
"You are not alone. Let us help each other."[3]

Which is more likely to attract participants who want to change? Which do you think will have a lot of self-pity involved in the sharing? These are the types of things you will want to consider. We did a quick search for support using words like *victim* or *survivor* in their titles and then searched for support without those types of words. Here is a sample of what we found from a group called *Physical & Emotional Abuse Support Group*:

> Life is not perfect, but it is getting there. I'm here to help other women, especially the young ones, understand that they are not alone and YOU can find the courage to make life become what YOU want. (MomOf4)[4]

> I happen to think that it is a form of abuse. Granted he doesn't hit you, but he is putting you down and disrespecting you. A person can only do to you the things that you allow them to do. (Wildcard)[5]

"I am so grateful for the information and support you provide online. I could have suffered for years or simply abandoned my relationship if I had not forced myself to act like I have a sense of self-worth. It hurt both of us, but letting my husband know my limits and boundaries gave him what he needed to be able to see himself, and I was able to support him through his own changes. I think, also, that I am very lucky. We seem to be okay now, and our future is full of possibilities."

—CARROL M.

The following sample came from a forum named *I Am a Victim of Verbal Abuse*, which was not as solution-oriented as the first.

"Misery loves company" and this is why they pick fights. I told my abusive OH that he is just like a bully. They pick a fight until you lose control and then make it your fault. Ugh. makes me sick to my stomach. I have ulcers already from my "eggshells." They are very clever at manipulating you. Mostly I just ignore him now or if I feel that I am going to lose it, I just calmly (or as calmly as possible) tell him that "I never argue with an idiot, they drag you down to their level and then beat you with experience" (AriesRSA).[6]

Not all posts are this clear cut. There is plenty of blaming and sympathy from all the sites, and there can be plenty of good advice on sites that use the words *victim, survivor,* and *inner child* in their titles and descriptions. Just be aware of these two basic orientations when addressing abuse. We hope you choose the type of support you can identify with and where you find encouragement to change. But you might feel you haven't reached the stage for tough solutions yet and still need personalized validation and sympathy until you are strong enough to change. This is your choice. Just be aware as you make it.

Join more than one group. You might consider joining both a forum and an email support group. The more help you get, the better. Shelly once sought information from Dr. Irene's verbal abuse website. She asked questions and sought answers. As a result, a young woman, Dawn, reached out and they became fast email friends—exploring the issues and growing together. Soon another woman asked to become part of the emails, and then another. As a result, they formed an email support group. In the beginning, their correspondence contained much complaining and blaming, but it soon emerged as a way to progress and support each other through the change. It led to the free online book *Email Trail of Self-Help*[7] and the website YouAreATarget.com to help the abused move away from the victim role they had become comfortable with. Group support is essential, but do not limit it to virtual support. Face-to-face support is essential also.

Choosing a Face-to-Face Group

Abuse has no particular preference for gender, wealth, race, religion, sexual orientation, education, or professional level. It can and does show up in just about any home or relationship imaginable. Additionally, abuse is not caused by a single factor. Even though we have encouraged you not to focus on why he abuses, choosing a support group is the one exception where knowing *why* he abuses might help you pick a support group that works for you.

When we have lost our way, we need help from like-minded women and men who have been suffering similar types of abuse and, more important, have learned how to make better choices. Often this will be a group that focuses on one particular aspect of our partner's abuse. For instance, Shelly's husband was verbally and emotionally abusive, and his most identifiable symptoms were rage, pornography, and exhibitionism. This greatly influenced the support groups that she chose, which included domestic violence support (because of his rage) and a 12-step group for the spouses of sex addicts.

"The best thing that ever happened to me was when he went into a rage and tore up the kitchen, forcing me to flee to the police. They couldn't do anything because he didn't hit me! But they sent me to a domestic violence group, and that group of women became my new family. I began to understand the pattern of control, disrespect, and humiliation this man used with me. I began to understand that I would never, never, never please him. Whether the windows were up or down didn't matter. This was not about me; it was about him and his anger."

—SHELLY M.

Location will also have a great deal to do with the program you choose. Many groups are simply not accessible where you live. Some of your help will be virtual (Internet) while you locate the most appropriate face-to-face groups available in your area. The community-based agencies will likely be professionally run talk therapies, while the 12-step groups will be self-help, based on working steps to change your behavior. All 12-step programs are free, and most municipal-run programs are based on income or are also free.

As a general rule, the self-help groups are based on learning about codependency and how to break free of those self-defacing behaviors. If possible, consider CoDependents Anonymous (CoDA) as your anchor group. They know what they are doing in terms of helping you find your way. In fact, they won't even let you talk much about what your abuser has done to you. They will want to hear about how you are dealing with it. Of course, if your abuser is an alcoholic, you will want to go to Al-Anon too. If he is a narcissist, you will want to find a support group for the co-narcissist. Here are some possibilities:

Program	Consider Using if	Contact
Al-Anon	Your partner drinks excessively.	al-anon.org
Battered Husbands Support	Your partner is female and abusing you. (Offers message board, chat room, and useful links.)	batteredhusbands support.com
CAIR (Changing Attitudes in Recovery)	You want specific techniques and tools that lead to better self-esteem. (Assistance in starting groups is available.)	cairforyou.com
Co-Anon Family Groups	Your partner uses cocaine, crack, or other drugs. (You can still join this group whether or not they are actively using.)	co-anon.org
COSA (Co-Sex Addiction)	Your husband engages in pornography, affairs, masturbation, and other sex problems.	cosa-recovery.org

Program	Consider Using if	Contact
CoDA (Codependents Anonymous)	You want to learn new behaviors no matter what the root causes are of your partner's maltreatment of you.	coda.org
Emotions Anonymous	You are experiencing emotional difficulties and want help specifically with that before evaluating whether you are ready to use the Respect-Me Rules.	emotionsanonymous.org
Gam-Anon Family Groups	Your partner has a gambling problem and it contributes to his abuse of you.	gam-anon.org
Domestic Violence Groups	You believe that your partner is on the verge of personal violence toward you and may have already shown aggression by hitting walls, breaking things, or hurting a pet.	Find through your local social service and human service agencies.
NarAnon	Your partner has a drug problem of any kind.	nar-anon.org
Recovering Couples Anonymous (RCA)	Your partner is on board and really wants to work with you so *he* starts respecting *you* and your boundaries. RCA is made up of couples committed to restoring healthy communication and developing a caring and functional relationship.	recovering-couples.org
S-Anon	Your partner has a sexual addiction. (Assistance available for starting groups. Similar to CoSA.)	sanon.org

"I recognize that much of my codependent characteristics were developed at an early age. I was raised in a family with mostly codependent women who had a difficult time teaching me how to be an emotionally and spiritually strong woman. I am a highly emotional individual, and as an adult, have found myself in relationships and situations that feed on my codependency. I am currently trying to leave a relationship with a man who has been diagnosed as a narcissistic sex addict."

—CARMEN B.

A manageable guideline for recovery programs is to use CoDA as your primary group for either virtual or face-to-face support. We encourage the combined use of lay support and professional help and recommend a minimum of three sources of support: online support, a face-to-face support group, and a therapist.

What to Do When He Accuses You of Betraying Him

The accusation that you are betraying him by seeking help is common. No doubt he has already accused you of betraying the relationship by having affairs, talking to your mother ("What happens at home stays at home"), hanging out with your friends ("If you loved me, you would want to be with me"), and so on. The accusation of betrayal is nothing new. It is simply a way for him to gain control, isolate you from outside influences, and make you feel as if you don't measure up. Whether or not you seek outside support, your abusive partner will accuse you of betraying him and the relationship through a hundred different ways. Since it's going to happen anyway, why not give it some teeth for such a good cause as reclaiming your life?

Chapter Highlights

You will need to cultivate the strong support of like-minded people who are working on solutions to reclaim their self-respect. The support can be either virtual (Internet) or face-to-face (community) groups. Make sure that your privacy is secure when you begin an email account for your virtual support. Your support should be three-pronged: virtual online groups, face-to-face local groups, and a one-on-one therapist.

Something to Think about

Helping others with their problems is often the best way to put your troubles in perspective. It can allow you to take a needed mental break from your own situation. You will find that it is easier to analyze others and what they are doing to keep themselves stuck than it is to see yourself. Not only will you get great feelings of worth and usefulness from offering to help others in your support group, but you will also undoubtedly gain a new awareness about yourself.

Notes

1. *Victims of Abuse Stand Up*, http://groups.yahoo.com/group/victimsof abuse/.
2. *Weasel Free*, http://health.groups.yahoo.com/group/weasel_free/.
3. http://health.groups.yahoo.com/group/womansemotionalabuse support/.
4. *Quality Health*, http://www.qualityhealth.com/physical-emotional-abuse-forum/introduction-1000001620.
5. Ibid.
6. "I Am a Victim of Verbal Abuse Forum," accessed September 26, 2010, http://www.experienceproject.com/stories/Am-A-Victim-Of-Verbal-Abuse/992170.
7. *Email Trail of Self-Help: Stopping Abusive Relationships*, http://www.youareatarget.com/trail.html. Also available at www.respectme rules.com/trail.pdf.

CHAPTER 11

Frequently Asked Questions

If you have a problem, you have a choice: You can either take care of the problem now, or suffer longer and still take care of the problem later. Either way you will take care of the problem eventually, or die from the pain.

—DOUG KELLEY, CH, CSL

THE USE OF THE ABUSE-STOPPING strategies presented in this book may necessitate a radical change in behavior and how you view your own role in a relationship. It is not easy to make major behavioral changes without encountering obstacles, problems, uncertainties, and complications. Although we have tried to make the information as user-friendly as possible in order to facilitate adopting the abuse-stopping techniques, real life is always more complicated than any "cookbook" approach would make it seem. To help readers navigate through the inevitable complications, the authors gathered up the most frequently asked questions and present their answers in this chapter. These are all actual questions that have come into www.YouAreATarget.com or have been asked in Dr. Marshall's private practice.

General Questions about Abuse

Q: What is the difference between anger and emotional/verbal abuse?

The frequency. A pattern of anger is abuse. Occasionally having a bad day or becoming very stressed and snapping at others is normal.

Q: *Most men think they are always right. It is the way men are. So is it still abuse?*

We certainly call a lot of things abuse, but *abuse* can be a relative term. Men don't always think they are right; they just want you to think so. That is beside the point. What he thinks is not for you to worry about, expose, try to change, or analyze. You need only decide how you will allow him to treat you and what you will allow him to say or not say to you. If you have any illusions that you can fix him, forget it. This is not about him, it's about you. You must decide how you will allow others to treat you and then set your boundaries and enforce them.

Q: *Am I wrong to feel so angry and hurt by my boyfriend's behavior?*

Feelings are not necessarily "wrong"; they are just a part of who we are. We must recognize, understand, and deal with them. We must learn to base our lives on what we do and on our behavior, not just on feelings. The pitfall here is that feelings can get us into so much trouble. We can learn to act our way into *feeling* good, but we often can't feel our way into *acting* good. Dwelling too much on your hurt feelings poses the danger of falling into the trap of feeling like a passive, abused victim. When it comes to abuse, it is better to focus on what steps you can take to stop it. So feel anything you want to. The important thing is to learn exactly what behavior you are willing to accept from your partner and do what is required to stop his abuse.

Q: *My wife doesn't do the verbal thing much anymore because she found out that I won't just lie down and take it, but she is still big into emotional and sexual abuse. Withholding sex for long periods of time (weeks) is her big attempt to control me nowadays. My question is, how do I set boundaries and consequences when the abuse is so passive-aggressive? She's not attacking me, she's just avoiding me.*

This is a good example of a situation that does not lend itself easily to a simple, formulaic, technique-driven answer. There are almost certainly some serious, deep-seated psychological issues at play. What are they? Impossible to say. I recommend therapy for this couple to help them sort it out. Here is the underlying dynamic that was uncovered with one couple I was working with in my own practice. The wife was using sex as a boundary (which I agreed was a healthy boundary in her case). Her husband's attitude was that she owed him sex as a wifely duty. Her attitude was, "No, it's my body. I'm only willing to be involved in intimacy with a partner whom I feel good about and lovingly toward. When we argue all the time and the air is filled with tension and hostility, I am not in an intimate mood and am not willing to go through the motions just to satisfy him. It makes me feel like I'm a prostitute to give him sex under these conditions, just because he wants it. I hate myself afterward and feel cheap and used." The solution for this couple was to first resolve their underlying marriage issues, and the intimacy naturally followed.

When partners avoid in an attempt to control, it is abuse. There are other ways to nurture yourself, however, when a partner avoids you—you can spend more time with friends, at the movies, with hobbies, and in support groups. You can't force them to want you sexually, and eventually you may have to make a decision on how you want to live your life in this relationship. But don't give up too quickly. Seek professional help and focus on what you can do for you, not how you can change them to meet your needs.

Q: If there is abuse occurring in a relationship, doesn't that mean there is an underlying problem that has to be addressed? How will the Miracle Principle and Respect-Me Rules fix the underlying problem? They seem too simplistic.

You are right. Abuse is a very complex issue. It is almost certainly multidetermined and full of complexities, like most human behaviors. There is no simple cure for abuse. These abuse-stopping techniques are meant to be a first step in repairing an abusive relationship. That is why we recommend therapy. Consider a medical problem. What does the ER physician do first? He stops the bleeding! The first step in repairing a broken relationship is to stop the abuse. It is toxic and injurious to your well-being. You don't deserve it, and nothing else will help while it continues. Once you have taken away the perverse satisfaction he gets from using you as his target, he will be left dangling, so to speak. In family systems theory, when you change your reaction to him, the normal pattern of the system has been upset. This creates an opportunity to take this "what do I do now? Everything's up in the air" tension and create a new, healthier interaction dynamic between you and him.

Questions about Reverse Abuse and Codependency

Q: My partner found pages that I had printed from your site. At first he was angry. The next morning, he gave me a hug and told me how sorry he was. Then he turned around and stated that there were some things that fit me from this article. Is this just another tactic, or can a victim take on some abuser traits in self-defense?

Yes, it is quite common for us to take on the traits of the abuser. We, at times, fight back hard, but then we are just playing into the dysfunction and become part of the problem, not the solution. You will not change him. In fact, it will just make the situation deteriorate (see Respect-Me Rule #12 from chapter 3). Whether you do to him what he does to you (hoping to show them what it's like and gain their sympathy) or take revenge, *you will never change an abuser.* You can only change your reaction and change how you allow others to treat you.

Some counselors ask their clients to "mirror" the behavior to their abuser. There was a school of thought that if an abuser could experience how it felt, he might be ashamed and want to change. The problem is, if someone has a personality disorder or is entrenched in blaming you, this absolutely will not work. It usually only works on rational people, and most abusers are not rational. As one of our website followers wrote, "It triggers their emotional immaturity and tit-for-tat attitude. In my case, my ex said, 'See I knew YOU were the abuser—not me. This proves it!' He just couldn't see his own abuse. He also engaged in PROJECTION— that is, projecting all his abusive habits on to me, which absolved him of the problem of dealing with or even facing his own abuse."

If you find yourself turning into a first-class witch in reaction to his abuse, which often happens if you are not physically afraid of him, then you need to concentrate on the Al-Anon principle of detachment (Al-Anons are the women who have learned how to live with alcoholism and are particularly good at pulling back and stopping their own insane reactions). Extreme reactions are common in response to feelings that you have not learned to deal with very well. You definitely don't want to take on the characteristics of your abuser. Detachment, as the Al-Anons put it, "is neither kind nor unkind. It does not imply judgment or condemnation of the person or situation from which we are detaching. It is simply a means that allows us to separate ourselves from the adverse effects that another person's alcoholism can have upon our lives."[1] In our case, we can substitute the word *abuse* for *alcoholism.* Learn all you can about detachment and how to apply it to your relationship, and don't become a hypocrite by doing the very things that cause you so much pain.

Q: Where do we draw the line at abuse? He calls my boundary-setting abuse. He says I abuse him because I don't respect him as he is. He accuses me of wanting him to change, or rather, trying to change him.

You absolutely *must* join a CoDA (codependency) group. Boundary-setting can be a tricky thing because, as you said, your abuser may claim you are abusive because you set boundaries. How can we tell the difference between manipulation and a personal boundary? Simple—you let go of the outcome regarding how he behaves and ensure the outcome of what you tolerate. In other words, he can yell and scream all he wants, but you will not be present to experience it if that is how he chooses to behave. A boundary is not intended to change him. It is a stand we take on how people treat us. Example: I won't be in a vehicle when someone continually drives too fast for the road conditions or over 80 mph. My boundary is safe driving. So if my partner chooses to drive 80 mph on our back country road, I will not be in the vehicle with him. He can do what he wants on his own, but if he does that with me in the car, I won't be in the car with him tomorrow. My boundary is designed to protect me, not change him.

Q: I controlled my *life by getting out of a relationship full of sickness. I had to control what my children are exposed to. I wasn't trying to control him, was I?*

You set the boundary describing what was acceptable for you to live with. Of course you were controlling. Not all control is bad. Is it bad to control your bowels? Is it bad to control what food you put in your mouth? Is it bad to control the influences you bring into your life? You may be overthinking your decision to protect yourself and your kids. Relax and share this concern with your support group. If you don't have a support group, even after leaving him is a good time to find one.

Q: Where does the line get drawn between abuse and looking after yourself? Where do we cross that line that says we are or are not codependent?

It is never abusive to take care of yourself and your children. A good guide for the "line" is this: Is this the next right thing? If you always do the next right thing, the thing you do will be right. It sounds simple and it is. And this means the next right thing for *you*, not them. Because when you do the right thing for *you*, it is the right thing for those around you. Here's an example. You've set a boundary and don't allow any source of pornography in your home—no magazines, Internet, phone sex, and so on. If the source is Internet, the consequence is to install a pornography filter. If pictures are found, they will be burned. If pictures are found a second time, they will mailed to your husband's pastor. If they are found a third time, separation papers will be filed. Is that the right thing to do? Yes, if it is the next right thing. Boundaries and consequences are the tool we use to enforce what is acceptable in our lives. So, is it the next right thing to set boundaries and enforce them against pornography? You answer. When he screams that you are a controlling, insane witch, that is his problem because you did the next right thing for you and your children.

Q: Does codependency parallel abuse?

The answer to your question is "definitely." They go together like a hammer and nail. Guess who's the nail? Codependents abuse themselves by denying their own needs and allowing themselves to be abused in a desperate attempt to "save" the object of their codependency. It gets even worse. The codependent often becomes so infuriated with the person who won't live up to her expectations that she lashes out in anger and ends up abusing him back. A pretty complicated mess, isn't it? Suffice it to say that codependency is no fun. It's imperative to recognize when it is occurring and work to correct it in order to get the relationship on a healthy and fulfilling track.

Q: I feel extremely angry at him so that sometimes I lie awake all night imagining that I am castrating him because he is so obsessed with himself and his "James Bond" looks. Is this normal? Is imagining him dead something I should seek help for?

Thoughts of revenge are normal. Acting upon them are not. It sounds like you are in the anger stage of abuse, from the target's perspective (see chapter 5). You can dissipate your anger by taking positive abuse-stopping steps to gain control of your own boundaries and life. If you are still consumed with thoughts of revenge, then professional counseling is in order.

Questions about Telling

Q: He says my telling was a bad thing. How do I get over the guilt?

Abusers always shift blame to the target, as you well know. Abuse seldom occurs in the open. In order to maintain an abusive relationship, one has to have secrets. Being private about aspects of your life is not the same as keeping secrets. They say we are only as sick as our secrets, and that is true. I, Shelly, did not start to recover until I told the secrets of my marriage—my husband's abusiveness and his sex secrets. Secrecy was a part of the sickness. Only in secrecy can abuse flourish in our society, and by keeping those secrets in our marriage, I kept us both sick. When I brought it out into the open, people could help me because they knew what was wrong, and my husband finally sought help for himself. Here is a quote from John Prin, author of *Secrets and How to Tell Them*:

> Clearly secrecy can debilitate character and judgment, and it can also lower resistance to the irrational and the pathological. "A stifling rigidity hampers those who become obsessed with secrecy," states Bok. "For them, it no longer serves sanity and free choice. Secrecy allows people to maintain facades that conceal. It shuts off the safety valve between the inner and the shared worlds."[2]

How to get over the guilt? *He* is not your conscience. As soon as you internalize the truth, you will know that what you did was right and guilt will fade. Think of this: if you kept his secrets and he molested a teenager, how would you feel? You know now that you did what was best for your inner self, your family, him, and the neighborhood. For me, it took two years to get over the same guilt feelings, but now I am grateful I told.

Q: *You say that keeping secrets is not good for the relationship, but my grandmother always said not to air our dirty laundry for the neighbors to see. I agree with her. After all, if I follow your suggestions and stay in the marriage, I don't want people thinking my husband is a bad man and that I was stupid to marry him. Would you?* (answered by John Prin)

The question you might ask yourself is, what is more important—my pride or the truth? If you are living with a man whom you know is leading a secret life, then others likely know it too (and it's not that much of a secret, is it?). So the "dirty laundry" is already out there and you are still hurting. When you hurt, you sometimes blame yourself and feel "stupid." If, however, you only suspect your husband of doing something in secret—pornography, drugs, gambling, an affair, whatever—then there's no need to hang out any dirty laundry. You can quietly investigate, or seek counseling, or start attending Al-Anon meetings, or read self-help books on the topic, or jot down his excuses and times/dates when you notice something suspicious. Also list your feelings at those times when you jot down a note. In time, you will have enough information to face the likelihood of confronting him privately with a plan in place about what to do regardless of how he reacts. A healthy relationship means both people must be healthy. Look to your own health first and don't let pride blind you or tell you lies.[3]

Questions about Therapy

Q: My psychologist thinks I should point out to my offender that his words are abusive, but I know he will just disagree or say that I am too sensitive, so I don't bother.

If you try to explain things and be reasonable, an abuser often twists your words and makes things worse. We know how humiliated you can feel when you say, "Stop calling me names. That's abuse," and he says something like, "You are so stupid that you don't even know what abuse is. If I say something that is true, that's not abuse. It's just a fact. If I called you a monkey, that might be abuse, but I called you fat; you *are* fat, so that's not abuse, is it?" So you don't engage with him. You don't explain and you don't defend. But if you say, "Name calling is abuse. You are calling me names. This conversation is over," then you are simply stating the facts to him. After the second statement, your offender will try to continue with something like, "It's over when I say it's over. You don't tell me when it's over!" If you are following the Respect-Me Rules, you are telling him that it's over *for you;* what he does is up to him. You are not engaged in the conversation any longer, and you enforce that boundary by not talking to him (leaving the area if you can) until he treats you with respect again.

Identifying abuse out loud can help in certain instances. It reminds *you* of what is going on. It reminds *you* that you have a boundary that must be enforced. If your abuser is seriously mentally ill or has no conscience, telling him he is being abusive will have little effect. However, if he is an abuser who got there because of his religion or culture or because you trained him that abusing you works, then there may be an advantage to pointing it out.

Q: How do I know I am not insane? After all, he leaves me question-ing my very being.

This is one reason we must not try to practice the abuse-stopping techniques until we have a support system in place. We all need people in our lives whom we respect and can use to bounce things off of. Support groups, both virtual and face-to-face, professional counselors, and friends you can trust will make all the difference. Your support system and your journal become an indispensable sanity compass.

Q: My therapist is teaching me how to stop antagonizing my hus-band. But I don't feel that I caused this at all like my husband says I have. My husband is the only one doing and saying mean and abusive things. What am I doing that makes him treat me this way?

It's not you, believe us! You might need a new therapist. Some therapists are not trained in abuse dynamics and cannot discern what is really going on. Remember that therapists can be taken in by an abuser's charm and manipulated just as you were in the beginning of the relationship. It is unlikely that your therapist will witness his abuse firsthand. The therapist must rely on what is said during a session. As a recipient of abuse that is now bad enough to warrant therapy, you are probably not the picture of health. You may be abrasive, hysterical, frazzled, and questioning your own sanity. If your therapist is not well-trained in emotional and verbal abuse issues, he will have a hard time effectively helping you.

For example, James, a therapist in Rapid City, was able to secure grant funds to run a domestic violence group for the abuser. Ironi-cally, he taught abusers how to ignore the triggers that their women "tempted" them with! James honestly believed that the women caused the abuse, and all he had to do was teach the guys to control their reactions while allowing them to believe that the women actually did things that caused it. Today James would not get a grant with that philosophical approach, but at that time, addressing domestic violence and abuse was in its infancy. Few professionals understood the dynam-ics. Fortunately, research is beginning to catch up to the practitioners, especially those professionals who have kept pace through workshops and continuing education in this area.

Insisting on your rights is paramount if you are going to be the winner in this life situation. Know that you don't deserve any kind of maltreatment from the one you love. Learn the skills needed to change the dynamics. In the meantime, find a therapist who is trained in domestic abuse so that you have a chance to save your marriage or move on to a healthier choice. Don't get trapped in the dark force of abuse.

Questions about Recovery

Q: I only recently realized I've been in an emotionally and psychologically abusive marriage for nearly twenty years. Can an abuser truly change lifelong behaviors? To me, it seems impossible because his abusive ways are literally who he is. If an abuser can truly change, what is the time frame?

This is an interesting question. Can an abuser really change? It depends. We suppose this is just the sort of answer you didn't want! Whether your partner can really change depends on why he is an abuser. There are many reasons, some as scary as brain chemistry, mental illness, and personality disorders, and some as simple as him coming from a culture or religion that accepts abuse as a part of male privilege. Patricia Evans says that occasionally some abusers are reformed and capable of change.[4] We have seen this miracle ourselves.

Of course, we don't know *your* partner. But if it is a brain chemistry problem such as a serotonin deficiency, maybe psychotropic medication could help. If it's his culture, he can learn to change, if he chooses to. If it's habitual, which some abuse is, he certainly can change his bad habits, but again, he has to choose to do so. If your partner learned that abuse worked because you responded to his abuse by doing what he wanted, then you certainly can teach him that it isn't going to work any longer. Under these circumstances, your offender might see the wisdom in working with you to attain an equal and rewarding partnership.

If, on the other hand, his abuse is the result of a personality disorder, it's problematic. We have seen remarkable changes once the woman changes. But Shelly can tell you that, in her own case, once she refused to let her husband abuse her by employing these techniques, he did stop. But she then lived with that hostility you hint of in your question. He didn't like it, but he didn't abuse her any longer because it failed to trigger the responses he wanted. However, since her husband didn't *really* change his character, only his immediate abuse of her, he finally demanded a divorce. We have found that if an abuser is not going to change, he usually finds a way to get out of the marriage so he can find someone else to abuse.

Q: Does it really take forever to recover? Will I ever feel normal again?

Yes, it probably does take forever. You will need to go through a CoDA program and have a support network for a very long time. Codependent targets need the support of a group of people whose goals and moral compass match their own. There is a two-year rule in mental health circles that professionals use as a guideline: You will probably need to be in a support group and with a therapist two years for every year that you were in an abusive situation. Whether you use CoDA, another 12-step group, a church organization, or something else, you may need it forever. Targets too easily slip back into old negative patterns. And about not feeling normal—don't worry about how you feel right now. Feelings improve over time, especially if you are behaving in a healthy manner. Basing action or decisions on how we feel is what gets us into the codependent behaviors in the first place. Base your decisions and actions on what you know in your head is right. You cannot *feel* your way into right actions. You have to *act* your way into right feeling.

Q: Recently, I tried to have a heart-to-heart conversation with my husband about how he is harming my health with all the stress, and the whole time I was talking, he sat at the dining table and doodled on a notepad. After he went to bed, I glanced at the notepad and saw that he had drawn a picture of my face with blood and wounds on it. He had written the words "AX TO FACE" next to the picture. When I confronted him about it the next morning, he laughed it off as a joke. I pray and hope that someday he will see value in me and treat me like the wife I try to be. I am always nervous about what will set him off. How do I deal with this type of threat? Am I really in danger?

There's a lot going on here. You definitely live with a classic abuser. When you hope someday he will see the value in you, you are asking for the impossible. These classic abusers seldom admit what they are doing or take any responsibility for their role. You seem to be making some classic mistakes too when you deal with him. Learning about abuse patterns, codependency, and self-respect will help you spot some of the problems between you and your spouse. For instance, you try to reason with him. Abusers aren't reasonable, because abuse is not reasonable. Confronting him may be assertive, but you are not setting boundaries and enforcing them. If you practice properly setting boundaries without trying to get him to understand why, you may make some progress. Usually when a target has a "reasonable" conversation about her partner's abusive behavior, she gives him ammunition to twist, deny, or minimize the problem or blame the target. It is usually best to enforce boundaries with a brief notice of what behavior is unacceptable. There is no real need to discuss why one won't accept maltreatment. It's not worth the target's time and usually just reengages her in the abuse.

We hope you saved the "AX TO FACE" picture. When he escalates to physical violence, you will need that for evidence to prove what you are living with. Threats of violence very often lead to violence. You could be in a very dangerous situation and should immediately contact a professional with the information of the drawing. In some states, that drawing is enough for police to press criminal charges. Don't take it as a joke. This type of threat is very serious. There is nothing funny about an ax to a face. Your life could be in danger. Please contact a domestic violence center immediately.

Questions about Blame

Q: What if he says I'm the one who is abusing him when he is actually abusing me?

This is a typical abuser tactic called blame-shifting. It is characteristic of an abuser to be in denial about his abuse and to blame others for his problems. Continue to enforce the Respect-Me Rules with their respective boundaries and consequences. What he says or believes is irrelevant to their effectiveness. Arguing with you is a trap. A target well versed in the Respect-Me Rules will simply move out of the way and let actions speak louder than words.

Q: Why do women stay? It seems like they must somehow like the abuse.

Reasons for staying are varied and often complex. Sometimes, they are as simple as wanting to stay with a man in order to reform him. Some women do it for the sake of the kids or because their religion dictates they stay. And some women love their husbands and figure leaving isn't the solution. Actually, the authors advocate staying in the relationship and trying to master the abuse-stopping techniques first. If they work, then the marriage is saved, which most people would agree is the optimal outcome. If they do not work but the target still stays, most people wonder why. We'll let the researchers answer that one. No matter who we stay with, it is a personal choice. Therapy might help a person make healthier decisions. The goal of this book is simply to offer some empowerment tools that help targets stop abuse within their relationship while improving their own self-worth and general state of happiness.

Questions about Your Approach

Q: What if I don't want to leave my husband? Is it possible to live successfully with an abuser?

As in the previous question, only you can answer that. What is your tolerance for pain? What is the cost/benefit of staying? If you want permanent relief from abuse, then you must eventually leave an abusive relationship. For the most part, an abuser is hell to live with, but it can be done somewhat successfully if he doesn't progress to physical attacks. Many online sources explore how to cope with an abuser. The suggestions may keep an abuser semihappy and at arm's length but will no doubt be hard on you. The suggestions are designed for relationships where no change is expected and the target just wants to make do, for any of a multitude of reasons. If this is the case, you might find some of them helpful, such as never disagreeing with him; acting awed by his achievements, good looks, and success; and being endlessly giving, patient, and there for him. You can practice most coping strategies and still enforce your Respect-Me Rules, so it may be worth it to you. But generally, the coping strategies leave you in a hollow and pointless relationship. That is why we don't teach the methods of coping. If you choose to stay, cope, and enforce boundaries, do not expect any long-lasting relief from abuse. Do make sure you find a good therapist that is trained in domestic abuse issues, and get a support group as a sanity barometer. An abuser can and will wear you out unless you inoculate yourself from their hurtful actions.

> "Sometimes we never let ourselves truly get away. We become convinced the abuse was deserved and feel guilty for not recognizing it for what it was and getting out sooner. Sometimes the damage goes so deep that leaving doesn't end the pain."
>
> **—SUSAN S.**

Q: What if you have set a consequence of

not being intimate with your husband when he has been abusive, but then he doesn't care that you are not giving him sex?

Use another consequence that he does care about. Not every consequence will work. You may have to use some trial and error.

Q: My domestic violence group keeps referring to us as survivors. I feel I survived my husband's abuse. Why do you say we are not survivors?

The words we use influence how we think and act. For instance, when caught doing something wrong, children often say, "He made me do it." We have to correct them by pointing out that they can choose their actions; others don't *make* them do things. This teaches children how to take responsibility for their own choices and learn how to control their own lives. Those who understand the dynamics of abuse can use that knowledge to take back control of their lives from the abuser. Using the word *survivor* denotes that we were victims of a larger force beyond our control, such as a plane crash. If one is raped, yes, she is a survivor. She did not choose anything. She is a victim of a heinous crime. But we do choose our partners. We are not talking about physical violence, which is something we may have little control over and of which we may indeed be a victim and survivor. But when it comes to verbal and emotional abuse, people have a lot more control than they realize. In almost all cases, they have the power to stop the abuser. What they lack are the skills to do so. Imagine standing in front of an archer as he pulls back the bow, aiming it straight for you. You can respond to this rather unfortunate situation by thinking either, "When the arrow hits, I will survive," or "I am a target." The latter thought demands evasive action. It puts us in control of our own destinies. If we don't want to be a target, we'd better get out of the line of fire. Think of yourself as a target, and the next time someone tries to abuse you, use the Respect-Me Rules and step out of the way.

Q: I tried several of the techniques years ago and found that it incited more violence. Recording conversations to expose the abuse, asserting yourself, and denying him control, in some instances, may get you killed. Sometimes you can't make it to the phone to dial for help. What do you say to this?

In severe cases like this, the best thing to do is get out of the relationship as quickly and safely as possible. Some people are sociopaths.

They care about no one but themselves and only desire power and control over others. They have no conscience and will use and abuse anyone who will stick around and allow herself to be exploited.

Questions about Helping

Q: How do I help someone in an abusive relationship?

It is a pretty helpless feeling to stand by and watch someone we care about being abused. In fact, according to some researchers, just watching others being assaulted, bullied, or sexually harassed is like breathing in secondhand smoke—it is not a neutral event. Dr. Richard J. Hazler, a Penn State researcher, says, "Our findings show that bystanders also experience moderate to severe psychological and physiological repercussions."[5]

One of the best places to start is understanding how abuse occurs in the first place. You must have three components:

1. Someone who is hurt by verbal and emotional maltreatment
2. One person who is perceived as more powerful than the other—a power differential. "I am right, you are wrong. I am the authority and you must obey. I control the money, you don't. I am better. You are beneath me."
3. Abuse in an ongoing pattern. The longer the abuse occurs, the more damage has been done.

We work on changing these dynamics by addressing all three. We help the person out of the victim role (being hurt) by understanding that she is a target, not a victim. Once she has had enough, she can make a choice whether to remain a victim and allow herself to be hurt or to do something about it. Next we change the power differential by giving the target the tools to build her self-respect and increase her personal power. These are the Respect-Me Rules, which, when enforced, empower the target to stop accepting unacceptable behavior. These rules break the destructive pattern as the target acquires the insight and skills to undertake this courageous life change.

You can help her understand the dynamics, encourage the use of new language to describe her situation, help her stop complaining about the abuse she allows, and encourage her to make choices about how she is to be treated. Know that she does not need rescuing. Help her develop resources (you being one) and a support system. Help her pick a counselor who understands abuse. Help her understand she doesn't have to live this way and that your concern doesn't mean you want her to leave her partner. What you want her to do is make her own decisions and regain her self-respect.

An abused person is often in an ongoing emotional crisis that prevents her from using her common sense and problem-solving abilities. You can greatly assist her by helping her understand the dynamics of abuse. Be a teacher, a cheerleader, and a coach. Be her nonjudgmental support and sounding board, and be there to help her take action once she decides to make change. If she chooses to stay in the relationship, don't take on the burden of thinking that you have failed her. Just as she can't change her abuser, know that you can't change her. You can be honest and you can be there. Beyond that, it is her choice.

Q: I admit that I am fairly unique. I am a male who is a victim of my wife's verbal abuse. I am looking for any kind of support, specifically websites for male victims of verbal abuse. Can you help me at all? I am in counseling, reading books, and so on. I am also religious and draw strength from my faith. I am attempting to now find my voice, which has been taken from me over the years. Any other ideas? Anywhere you would suggest I go?

As much as you may feel alone, you are not unique. There are plenty of women who abuse men, and it's difficult for the man to come forward because he is supposed to "be a man." Most help books, websites, and literature on verbal abuse present the abused woman's point of view. We most often hear about males abusing females. However, there is plenty of abuse to go around, and female partners are certainly just as capable of dishing out the abuse.

These Respect-Me Rules are designed to work in either direction. Dr. Irene's verbal abuse website (www.drirene.com) offers many good suggestions for men. Men, including a judge, who are abused by their wives write columns and answer inquiries. You can examine how codependency may be part of the problem. There is also a domestic abuse help line for men on the Web at batteredmenshelpline.org, which is a set of links and resources for men who are victims of domestic violence or abuse. The site offers statistics on domestic violence against men, alternative thoughts about domestic violence in general, and referrals to domestic violence shelters that accept men. If you are ready to make a commitment to enforce the Respect-Me Rules, you are ready for change.

Notes

1. West Virginia Alanon/Alateen, *Detachment*, accessed September 25, 2010, http://wv.al-anon.alateen.org/detachment.html.
2. John Prin, "Are Secrets Good or Bad?" *John Prin Articles,* accessed February 10, 2010, http://www.johnprin.com/articles/art-secrets-goodorbad.htm. Appeared in *The Phoenix*, (St. Paul, February 2004).
3. John Prin, *YouAreATarget.com*, http://youareatarget.com/faq.html#5._You_say_that_keeping_secrets_is_not.
4. Patricia Evans, chapter 12 in *Verbal Abuse Survivors Speak Out on Relationship and Recovery* (Avon: Adams Media Corporation, 1993).
5. Paul Blaum and Vicki Fong, "Impact of repeated abuse can be as severe for bystanders as victims." *Penn State Live*, accessed September 26, 2010, http://live.psu.edu/story/9438.

How to Spot an Abuser on the First Date

The reason it is possible to spot an abuser fairly early on is that most abusive relationships tend to follow a fairly standard formula. Most abusers are very similar and act in similar ways, and while they are actually very clever, their predictable nature can often give them away.

—MACK LEMOUSE

IT WOULD BE NICE IF ABUSERS had one easily identifiable feature that would broadcast a loud and clear message to others such as, "Unless you are a masochist and want to be abused, belittled, and exploited for my own selfish edification, then stay away from me." Unfortunately, it's not that easy to spot them. Successfully identifying abusers requires, at a minimum, knowledge of their common characteristics and careful observation plus vigilance on the part of potential targets. Abusers come in many varieties, and some are very clever at disguising their underlying toxic personality. However, they do share some common characteristics. We will present the research findings along with some astute observations from those who have been in the trenches.

Can you always spot an abuser early on?

No, of course not. Yet most abusers carry into the relationship an underlying pathos that lies in wait for the right opportunity to express itself. In new relationships, there is often an initial euphoria that masks any darker undertones. Theoretically, it is possible for abuse to "appear out of nowhere," such as in cases of disease (brain tumors or enceph-alitis), an emerging mental illness (psychosis or dementia), medical problems (chronic pain or an addiction), or severe trauma in which the stressed person lashes out at others in a type of post-traumatic reaction (think of a partner returning from war).

France is the first country in the world to ban psychological vio-lence between married and live-in couples. Under the new law, it is a prosecutable crime to insult, yell at, and sling curses and vile names at your partner. The law is aimed at protecting women from abuse because the French are aware that most physical abuse starts out as verbal and emotional abuse.[1] This is good news for French targets. The Respect-Me Rules are now backed up by the weight of law!

Unless you live in France, using this law is not an option. Another step you can take to inoculate yourself from abuse is to learn the common characteristics of abusers *before* you pick a partner. If, after using the Respect-Me Rules, you find that you are alone, your abuser didn't change, or he didn't want you once you stood up to him, then it is time to identify the potential controller *before* you fall in love again. Study the list below if you are back looking for a partner but truly don't want to end up with another one like the last. Learn to identify how an abuser behaves, what he talks about, and what he focuses on right from the start.

Unfortunately, not all abusers will exhibit the following signs. Those who end up as abusers because of culture or religion will exhibit some of these signs, especially the ones that stem from male privilege. The abusers who have person-ality disorders (narcissists and borderlines) and full-blown mental illness (psy-chopaths) are more likely to show these signs from day one. The abusers least likely to show these red flags at the beginning of a relationship are those who are basically taught by their partners that abuse works. They may

> "He goes into detail about what is and what is not love. I think I have a lot of inner healing to do, and I'm not banking on a relationship right now because I don't want to get sucked into that again. Yuck. Not only do I need to heal and deal with childhood issues, abuse from a new man on top of that is definitely a nightmare. Thanks for your work."
>
> **—ANDREA G.**

have begun as pretty normal partners and slowly learned that if they get mean, their partners do what they want. Nevertheless, most abusers do follow a recognizable pattern of behavior almost from the first date.

Abusers want to *gain control* and *be superior*. As your relationship progresses, you will soon be made to feel inferior if the abuser gets his way. But the caveat is that in the beginning, he can be charming and attentive. The only way for an abuser to get in good with you from first contact is to make you feel very special. "What," you may ask? "An abuser is going to make me feel special? That's counterintuitive."

"They con us with promises of love and care taking. Thieves and con men can be brought to justice for stealing money or goods. Why is there no justice to punish the ones who steal our chances at happiness?"

—SUSAN S.

Abusers start off making you feel like one in a million.

There are two types of individuals that make you feel like one of a kind, as if fate has conspired to bring you together—your one and only soul mate, or your worst nightmare: an abuser. While your soul mate is looking to bring love and fulfillment into your life, an abuser is looking to control your life. They aren't always easy to tell apart. At first blush, both make you feel special. You must go into the first few dates with your eyes open. Then the defining differences become quite clear.

First, an abuser will sweep you off your feet. You are the best thing that has ever happened to him. He is eager and excited and proclaims that fate brought you together. Of course, if truth be told, he proclaims this to everyone. He compliments you profusely and cannot believe he is so lucky. He gazes into your eyes, kisses your hands. Nothing is too good for you. He has found what he was looking for, all within a ridiculously short period of time.

Any rational person would recognize that this is fantasy, not fate. But people, especially women, are primed to believe in love at first sight, fated soul mates, and incurable romance. We want to believe in such fantasies, and therefore someone who wants you as his very own target knows what to say to hook you.

Michelle from northern Idaho is a prime example. She met Kurt, who courted her for a few days. He was attractive and attentive but quite overwhelming. From their first meeting, *before the first date*, Kurt tried to pressure Michelle to go up to the mountains to spend time alone with him. He told her how special she was, how they would be great together, how she was everything he ever dreamed of, and all the lovely things women want to hear. About the time she was going to accept his offer, he was already seeing Kathy, her best friend. They became a couple almost overnight. Michelle was baffled because Kurt truly seemed infatuated. How did Kurt switch true loves so fast? Michelle thought it must have been because her friend was cuter and more petite, and since they were best friends, they shared traits that Kurt was attracted to. It made sense. She wasn't moving as fast as Kathy had, so she lost this really cute guy to her friend.

What neither Michelle nor Kathy understood was that Kurt was a classic abuser. If they had known the signs, both would have figured out immediately that he was not a good choice. Very early on in the relationship, he started preventing Kathy from going anywhere alone and called her vile names when they fought. He began living off of her. She couldn't even look at another guy without Kurt accusing her of betraying him. Kathy woke up in a nightmare, and it took her several years to maneuver back out of the relationship.

Michelle's hesitation is what saved her. Kathy was a more willing target at that time and paid a huge price. Here are some things that you can identify from the very first date:

He is eager to start the relationship.

- You are cast in the role of the love of his life almost immediately.
- He may talk of marriage and kids right away ("We'd make beautiful babies together.")
- He assumes there will be a second date. After all, you are meant to be together.
- He may pressure you for sex on the first date.
- He refers to your "relationship" on the first date.
- He calls immediately after the first date, usually before you hit the pillow, sends gifts, and shows up at your work because you are now a couple.

He encourages a feeling of danger and power about himself.

- He may stockpile and collect weapons, talk incessantly about them, spend a lot of time practicing martial arts, or engage in weapon activities such as target practice. He lets you know that he is prepared for anything (famine, crisis, survival, civil war).

- He goes out of his way to be rude and condescending to service people (a cab driver or a waitress), gets a kick out of their discomfort, and then may leave a lavish tip to impress you (both behaviors show a need to be powerful and in control).

- He exhibits road rage.

- He drives fast and recklessly.

- He clenches his fists when frustrated, perturbed, trying to get his way, or thwarted.

- If he has pets, it is likely to be something dangerous like a python (they love the power it conveys). He may have a pit bull, wolf breed, or other aggressive breed of dog.

- If he has a dog, the dog is highly controlled (chained outside to a stake, not allowed in the house, or never allowed in the bed). An abuser doesn't seem to mind making the pet uncomfortable in ways such as leaving it outside in extreme weather or leaving it alone for long periods.

- He admits he has a problem, such as being an ex-con or having a history of sex addiction, gambling, drugs, or alcohol, but says it is "handled" now because he found a new life with Alcoholics Anonymous and brags about his newfound spiritual self. "You wouldn't want to have known me then," he whispers as he sets a dramatic tone, suggesting he was so dangerous then.

- He lets you know or suggests that he has killed someone or would kill someone for you. Often this is in connection with the military, but if he is bringing it up during the first few dates, he is showing you how powerful he is. Or he may suggest that he was in the Mafia and say, "In order to keep you safe, I can never tell you the things I did." Normal men don't brag about people they killed or may kill when they are trying to impress a new love. Normal men don't want to scare you. Abusers do.

"He does have the ability to be nice and respectful and considerate and mature and loving, or am I wrong? Does he not have this capacity, because he was that way with me for a long time, and he is able to be that way with others. Or is it a fraud show?"

—MARTHA L.

He seems commanding and takes charge—in other words, he is a compulsive controller.

- He insists you ride in his car or that he drives your car and holds onto the keys.
- He orders for you from the menu, picks the restaurant, or tells you to pick but then turns up his nose at anything you suggest and makes the decision anyway (this also includes movies and other activities).
- When you return from the restroom, he interrogates you (asks why you took so long and who you saw).
- He exhibits a need to outfox others. He brags about how he pulled one over on someone, outsmarted the cop, hid assets from his ex-wife, didn't pay all his taxes, and so on.
- You notice possessiveness and posturing toward any man that may notice you (he pulls you to a private table away from the bartender so he can "have you to himself").
- He tries to enlist you in getting revenge on or embarrassing his ex by having you show up with him at a party or place where she works, and he takes delight in her discomfort.

He makes you feel extraordinarily special (before he could possibly know who you are).

- He confides in you and claims he's already told you things he's never told anyone else. He doesn't know why, but he already feels that comfortable with you. It seems like he is really sensitive and open. He may even tell you some deep, dark secret. It's just a technique. Every woman in his life has heard this.
- He claims you already understand him better than any other woman in his life.

- He tells you how "good" you make him feel. (Later he will tell you how "bad" you make him feel).
- The term *soul mate* immediately emerges, or he says something like, "I think I have always loved you, but just didn't know where to find you," or more subtly, "I need someone to complete me." Then he stares at you as if you are definitely the one. He may expect his partner to meet all his needs. This sounds romantic at first, but "You're all I need" turns quickly into "I need you all the time and I am all you need," and life becomes unbearable.
- He seems very interested in hearing all about you but interjects things about himself frequently to show how much you are alike (if you love fish, he loves fish, or you both like sci-fi, have conservative views, and so on). This is called mirroring. He points out similarities to show compatibility and prove that you are meant for each other. Later you will be expected to be interested in everything that interests him, and anything you like will then be ignored and put down.
- His act seems a little too polished, and he shows larger-than-life demonstrations of devotion and being "wowed" by you.
- He may proclaim that he thinks you are his last and best chance at love. If it doesn't work with you, it won't work with anyone. (He actually says this to everyone he targets).
- If he is at all sophisticated, he will admit to some personal problems but demonstrate how he is working on himself (he'll mention the book *Men Are from Mars and Women Are from Venus* or talk about Dr. Phil's sage advice that he is following) and imply that since you understand him so well, you both may enhance each other's growth.
- He says you kiss better than anyone he's ever kissed before.

He is artful at blaming others.

- He may blame all his previous relationship failures on the woman he was with, claiming that she was controlling (projection) or only wanted him for his money (even if he doesn't have any). He may call her neurotic, a man-hater, a "feminazi," a manipulator, and selfish. According to him, she simply wanted a meal ticket or she tried to "take him" in the divorce. The court sided with her because she lied or, conversely, he outsmarted her because he was more clever than her and her attorneys. You can see that what he did was unfair, but he delights in it.

- He complains about how his mother damaged him.
- Any job he lost was "their" fault. Foreclosure was "her" fault. Lack of recognition was because others unfairly ruined his credibility.
- He explains how the cops had it out for him and set him up.
- He has a tendency to blame every failure or mishap on others or the government. He doesn't assume personal responsibility for anything. He blames you, the cab driver, the waitress, the weather, or the government for his problems. For example, he claims it was a speed trap, not that he was driving fifteen miles an hour above the speed limit. Or, "Why didn't you tell him the exit was just ahead?"

He is self-centered.

- Even if he's asking about you, he constantly shifts the conversation back to himself and blames or brags. There is no real reciprocal conversation.
- He is very offended if you take a phone call while on a date with him, even if it is your children, and especially if it is a business call.
- He is hypersensitive and quick to feel slighted, injured, and insulted.
- He is impatient in lines, in traffic, when you need to use the restroom, or if you want to shop for something.
- He may try to pressure you into immediately dropping everything to spend more time with him (even though you have kids at home to take care of) or taking the day off work to spend it with him. If you point out you have a job, he will say, "I can take care of you. Don't worry about your job."

There are many red flags that denote an abusive mind-set, but these are the ones that are likely to show up in the first few dates. Making you feel special during courtship is something that definitely does not last with an abuser and only returns during the honeymoon stage of abuse. If you truly don't want to subject yourself to the possibility of abuse, the above are glaring red flags. The warning here is that if you don't see how the above signs could possibly be bad in a new relationship, then you probably will find yourself in another such relationship.

Our suggestion is to carefully go over each of the above *before* a first date. If you find yourself saying the above red flags don't apply to your situation and you still believe that this relationship is meant to be, you are in trouble. Recently Shelly found it quite easy to identify an abuser who asked her out. Her potential date told her quite candidly that he was schizophrenic and said, "Don't worry, I'm not dangerous." He told her that he lived with his mother until she died last year and that he had the good kind of schizophrenia, where the voices just told him "about spiritual things."

Recognizing red flags as obvious as the above doesn't require much skill. No, Shelly did not even go out on a first date with this man. But a few years ago, when she met a good-looking veteran, she fell hook, line, and sinker for these lines: "You have brought me out of a twenty-year depression. You kiss better than anyone has ever kissed me before. We fit so well together—like God made us for each other. You are everything I ever dreamed of. Nothing is too good for you." Fortunately, she was enforcing all the Respect-Me Rules, and the relationship only lasted a few months. Once this man found that he could not call her names, throw fits when he was frustrated, disappear without a word when he was mad, get Shelly to pay for everything, or isolate her from her family, he told her, "This is not working out for me." The week before, he had been talking marriage. This relationship demonstrated the real value of self-respect and demanding respect from a possible partner. Although she may have been hoodwinked in the beginning, it did not last long.

Do Your Detective Work

Ask others what they know about your new love interest. What's his reputation like? Does he have a criminal record? Has he been divorced multiple times or had a slew of restraining orders taken out against him for domestic violence? Also listen to your intuition. If you have any qualms, simply Google his name. All kinds of facts pop up, such as past court cases or an entry on a sexual offender's list. Look at his MySpace or Facebook page. Do disturbing words or pictures appear? Do their pages scream "Me! Me! Me!" or do you see a caring man who pays attention to his friends and family? For a modest fee, you can even go so far as to order a net-based background check.

Remember, people are on their best behavior for a first date. They are motivated to show their best side, so that is the very best you will ever see of that person. If any of the above warning flags appear under conditions where he is most likely trying to keep his negative

> "At domestic abuse counseling they are adamant that they do not change, cannot change. My faith tells me otherwise, but, in truth, he got me by fraud. If he had been honest, I would never have dated him, let alone married and had a child with him."
>
> **—CANDY GIRL**

qualities under wraps, imagine how magnified those behaviors will become when he is stressed and has lost the motivation to present himself well.

If you see one or a few of the above qualities on a first date, beware. If you see more than that, be forewarned. Seeing several signs is a clear red flag. Stay alert for the abuse signs and signals in all your significant relationships. If they start to appear regularly or with increasing intensity, you know what to do. Whip out your abuse-stopping strategies and let your date know in no uncertain terms that you respect yourself and demand respect from others. If he takes the hint and responds, great. There may be some potential there. If not, it means your date is more committed to his abusive ways than he is to you. Run!

Being Forewarned Is Being Forearmed

When forewarned with knowledge and vigilance, it is possible to root out a large percentage of potentially toxic partners and avoid future grief. It all starts with self-knowledge. Those who self-examine and gain insight into their own subconscious motives and neurotic needs will have an advantage in avoiding relationship train wrecks. Not that knowing why you have neurotic needs will stop abuse, but it certainly can give you a foundation for questioning who you are attracted to and challenging yourself to make better choices.

For instance, do you have an unconscious need to "fix" obviously impaired significant others? That's a good neurotic need to investigate. Maybe low self-esteem distorts the way you see and approach life. You may think, "I don't deserve to be treated well." or "Who else would want me?" If you understand yourself, you can understand why the Respect-Me Rules feel so uncomfortable. An awareness of your limitations coupled with the red flag warnings for the first date may help you avoid that self-centered, controlling jerk and choose instead the spectacularly fulfilling, symbiotic relationship of your dreams.

Many people call it fate when you find that perfect someone and live happily ever after. What about the authors of this book? We are incurable *respect* romantics; we call it romance only when you teach that perfect someone *how you want to be treated*.

Chapter Highlights

Here are some characteristic red flag warnings that often appear on the first date:

- He exhibits excessive eagerness.
- He encourages an air of danger and power about himself.
- He seems commanding and takes charge. In other words, he is a compulsive controller.
- He makes you feel extraordinarily special before he could possibly know who you are.
- He is artful at blaming others.
- He is extremely self-centered.

Something to Think about

Don't take these warning signs lightly. If you find yourself saying, "Yes, but . . . " repeatedly as you read the above signs, STOP and think about what that means. If you find yourself deliberately NOT reading the above signs before a date, think again about what that means. We are talking about your welfare, your self-respect, and your happiness. Even though no single characteristic points to an abuser and you can't jump to conclusions based on one or two red flags, you must pay attention to your intuition—your gut feelings, the little twinges of uneasiness. Mack LeMouse, an author for HealthGuidance.org, writes, "Unlike an abusive partner then, you should always give value to your emotions. They are there to guide you, and whether other people understand them or not they are valid and important. At the end of the day a relationship is meant to make you feel good about yourself and increase your self-esteem."[2]

Notes

1. Henry Samuel, "Husbands can be jailed for insulting wives under new French law." *Telegraph*, accessed September 26, 2010, http://www.telegraph.co.uk/news/worldnews/europe/france/7863702/Husbands-can-be-jailed-for-insulting-wives-under-new-French-law.html.
2. Mack LeMouse, "Emotional Abuse—Are You Being Too Sensitive?," *Health Guidance*, http://www.healthguidance.org/entry/12781/1/Emotional-Abuse--Are-You-Being-Too-Sensitive.html.

Abuse Slogans

THE FOLLOWING IS A LIST of slogans that will help remind you of your new choices and responsibility. You can copy these or put them on Post-it notes around your home as reminders of your new life and use them in conjunction with Respect-Me Rule #11: Use a Prompt. Read them all and then use the ones that resonate within. Review them every few months. You will find that as you grow and change, new slogans resonate. They will not all have meaning for you at the same time. This is because learning to respect yourself and stop abusive treatment is a process. Your awareness of it changes as you change.

- A loss in life is not a loss of life.
- Act, don't react.
- ALL "shoulds" are a lie.
- "No" is a complete sentence.
- Allowing abuse is self-abuse.
- Bullyproof yourself.
- Change only happens when the pain of holding on is greater than the fear of letting go.
- Choice, not chance, determines destiny.
- Come out of the closet; you've been hung up long enough.
- Crazy-making is what you make of it.
- Detach, don't disappear.
- Detachment is neither kind nor unkind.
- Don't "should" on yourself.
- Enforce the Respect-Me Rules.
- Feelings are not facts.

- Formula for failure: try to please everyone.
- How you respond is your responsibility. How they respond is their responsibility.
- What would an adult do in this situation?
- I deserve more.
- I matter.
- If nothing changes, nothing changes.
- If I always have to walk on eggshells around my partner, that's "fowl" play.
- If you are constantly being mistreated, you are probably co-operating with the treatments.
- If you don't change, nothing changes.
- In order for someone to give you a bad day, you have to take it.
- It takes two to tango.
- It's not your business to keep their secret.
- It's not "Don't take it out on your partner." It's "Don't take it in."
- Keeping his secret keeps you sick.
- Know your no's.
- Letting go is not caring for, but caring about.
- Make it happen.
- No abuse excuse!
- Nobody gives you a bad day without your permission.
- Not being able to ask for support is a real sign of weakness.
- Our background and circumstances may have influenced who we are, but we are responsible for who we become.
- Pain heals; abuse scars.
- People don't walk over you until you lie down.
- Practice makes it better.
- Refuse to be abused.
- Refuse to star in his psychodrama.
- Never take yourself too seriously!
- See patterns and choose change.
- Self-respect is the most important respect you can earn.
- Set boundaries; keep boundaries.
- Stay put and act in your own best interest.
- Take the bully by the horns.
- The bigger the secret, the more dangerous.

- The reason people blame other people is that there is only one alternative.
- The worst abuse excuse: it's not that bad yet.
- Today I have a choice!
- Today, take care of yourself. Tomorrow you can worry about them.
- Walking on eggshells is for the birds.
- When the horse dies, dismount.
- Who is your priority?
- You'd better stop pleasing the abuser, because he cannot be pleased. You'd better start pleasing yourself because then at least someone will be pleased.

Tips for Enforcing Boundaries

Why set boundaries?

- To preserve your self-respect and integrity.
- To maintain your autonomy and protect who you are.
- To establish how you allow others to treat you.
- To maintain healthy relationships with yourself and others.

Respecting yourself is your job.

- Live your life based on principles, not personalities.
- Respect yourself because you do the right thing.
- Determine what behaviors and treatment you will and will not accept from others.
- Don't compromise on your values and morals.
- Don't let anyone put you down for your moral and religious beliefs.
- Although tolerance is admirable, don't hang out with people who do not share your values.
- Learn to say no.

Boundary-Setting Template

1. Pause and Choose

Choose to demand respect. Make a choice: Am I going to allow this person to continue to abuse me, or will I enforce the Respect-Me Rules?

2. Set Boundaries

Describe the specific offending behavior. Do not speak in generalities. State that the behavior, action, words, or intent is something you consider abusive. State clearly that if it continues, there will be consequences.

3. Implement Consequences

If he continues with the unacceptable behavior, the consequences have to be appropriate and reasonable and something you are willing to enforce.

"If you do this . . ." (Describe in detail what they are doing that you find unacceptable.)

"I will . . ." (Tell them exactly what you will do, including the time frame.)

"If you continue this behavior . . ." (State the action you will take if the first consequence is ineffective.)

Don'ts of enforcing boundaries with verbal and emotional abusers:

- Don't ask, "Why did you say that to me?" Never question why he abuses; it gives him an opening to abuse you further.
- Don't say, "That hurts my feelings." He wants to hurt your feelings, so you would just be rewarding him.
- Don't psychoanalyze him and try to figure out why he is the way he is. It doesn't matter why. Finding out why is your attempt to fix him. You need to figure out why you allow it and fix that.
- Don't set a boundary you don't really mean. If you are not willing to enforce a limit consistently, it makes your abuser worse, not better. Later your boundary will be harder to enforce when you do mean it.
- Don't compromise on abuse. Abuse is not negotiable. It has to be stopped—period. Compromising on abuse is like saying, "You called me a pig, but I'm a reasonable person, so let's compromise. Just call me a piglet." You compromise on differences of opinion, not mistreatment.
- Don't answer questions that come from his abuse state (questions that involve accusations, guilt, and blame). Just because someone asks a question does not mean you have to answer it. If you feel you must say something, say, "I don't answer questions designed to hurt (or humiliate, manipulate, anger, or berate) me. We will talk only when you talk to me like an adult (or loving spouse, equal, friend, or caring partner).

- Don't enforce a boundary if you are afraid he will hurt you. Do not allow yourself to be in an unsafe situation. If the abuse gets physical or you are afraid, trust your gut! Do not rationalize fears of safety away. Deep inside you know if your partner is capable of or has contemplated hurting you or your kids. Consider leaving and getting help if this is the case. Call the police if he threatens violence. It is a crime.

Believe in your boundaries; believe in yourself.

Practice these assertive statements:

- This is what I will do (describe the action). This is what I won't do (describe the action).
- I do not allow others to treat me as an object.
- I do not allow others to call me names.
- I do not allow others to humiliate me.
- I do not participate in sexual acts that make me uncomfortable.
- I do not hang around others who give me the silent treatment or ignore me.
- I'm not responsible for the happiness of any other person than myself.
- I refuse to be manipulated.
- It is not me who makes others angry; only they can make themselves angry.
- I have the right not to participate in conversations if I don't want to.
- I will only participate in conversations if I feel safe.
- I will only participate in conversations if I am addressed in an adult manner.
- I'm not responsible for fixing others' problems.
- I do not need to make excuses for other people, especially if it involves me.
- Expect me to tell others if I am being abused in any way.
- Although I believe in keeping private things private, abuse that is kept private becomes the weapon of the abuser. I expose abuse.
- Secrets that shield abusers are a form of enabling. I don't keep them.
- I am responsible for the company I keep.

- I am responsible when I accept abusive behavior.
- I do not answer questions designed to hurt, humiliate, or degrade me.
- I do not have to answer a question just because someone asks me something.
- I am not responsible for making anyone angry.
- I can't make another person happy or keep him happy.
- I can make my own decisions, but if I want another's input, I'll ask.
- I can't help my partner stop abusing. I can only tell him what I will and will not allow around me.
- I can respond calmly.
- If I am afraid of my partner and afraid to enforce my boundaries, something is terribly wrong.
- If something is terribly wrong, I will seek professional (and, if necessary, legal) help.

LIST OF QUOTATIONS

Chapter 1
"Harvey Fierstein Quotes." *Brainy Quote*, accessed September 24, 2010, http://www.brainyquote.com/quotes/quotes/h/harveyfier101058 .html.

Chapter 4
"Types of Domestic Abuse," *Hidden Hurt*, http://www.hiddenhurt .co.uk/Types/faces.htm.

Chapter 5
"The Cycle of Abuse," *Heart2Heart*, http://www.heart-2-heart.ca/ women/page5.htm.

Chapter 6
Quote on p. 71 found in Phillip McGraw, PhD, *Relationship Rescue: A Seven-Step Strategy for Reconnecting with Your Partner* (New York: Hyperion, 2000), 65–6.

Quote on p. 72 found in Irene Matiatos, "Just Exactly What Is Codependence?" *Dr. Irene's Verbal Abuse Site*, http://www.drirene.com/ coinfor.htm.

Chapter 7
Pamela Brewer, MSW, PhD, LCSW-C "Dealing with Emotional Abuse," accessed August 30, 2010, http://larryelder.warnerbros.com/emotional_abuse.html.

Chapter 8
John Howard Prin, "Are Secrets Good or Bad?" *John Prin Articles*, accessed February 10, 2010, http://www.johnprin.com/articles/art-secretsgoodorbad.htm. Appeared in *The Phoenix*, (St. Paul, February 2004).

Chapter 10

Jeanne King, PhD, "End and Heal from Emotional Verbal Abuse—Recognize It's Not about You," accessed September 25, 2010, http://www.preventabusiverelationships.com/emotional_verbal_abuse.php.

Chapter 11

Doug Kelley, CH, CSL, "Empowered Recovery." *Selected Alcoholic Relatuionship Questions Answered*, http://www.empoweredrecovery.com/articles/advice.htm.

Chapter 12

Mack LeMouse, "Emotional Abuse—Are You Being Too Sensitive?" *Health Guidance,* http://www.healthguidance.org/entry/12781/1/Emotional-Abuse--Are-You-Being-Too-Sensitive.html, (accessed March 2, 2010).

ABOUT THE AUTHORS

MICHAEL J. MARSHALL, PhD, and SHELLY MARSHALL, BS, CSAC, are a brother and sister team who have dedicated over thirty years to working with people in recovery from addictions, dysfunctional family issues, and abusive family patterns.

Michael is a research psychologist and private practitioner who teaches his clients how to recognize and break free from the abusive cycle, which is particularly endemic in his home state. He is the author of the acclaimed parenting book *Why Spanking Doesn't Work: Stopping This Bad Habit and Getting the Upper Hand on Effective Discipline* (Bonneville Books, 2002) and numerous journal articles.

Shelly has expertise in addictions, and her work in law enforcement has given her experience with abusive family situations and domestic disputes. In recent years, due to her personal experiences with an abusive husband, she became involved in Virginia's Domestic Violence programs as an advocate for victims. She has been published in recovery periodicals and local Virginia papers with her exposés and self-help articles regarding spousal abuse matters. She is the author of *Day by Day* and *Young, Sober & Free* as well as other popular self-help books.

The Marshall team is well known in the family, addictions, and mental health fields, making them the perfect team to offer the Respect-Me Rules approach to elimination of verbal and emotional abuse.